my life as a
traitor

ZARAH GHAHRAMANI was born in Tehran in 1981. She is now permanently resident in Australia. This is her first book. Her co-writer, Robert Hillman, was born in 1948 and grew up in rural Victoria. He has written several novels as well as poetry and short fiction. His 2004 memoir, *The Boy in the Green Suit*, won Australia's National Biography Award.

This book is dedicated with love and esteem to my friend Akbar Mohammadi, whose bravery, which so greatly exceeded my own, cost him his life.

my life as a traitor

zarah ghahramani

with robert hillman

BLOOMSBURY

LONDON · BERLIN · NEW YORK

First published in Great Britain 2008
This paperback edition published 2009

Copyright © Zarah Ghahramani and Robert Hillman 2007

The moral right of the authors has been asserted

No part of this book may used or reproduced in any manner whatsoever
without written permission from the Publisher except in the case of brief
quotations embodied in critical articles or reviews

Bloomsbury Publishing Plc
36 Soho Square
London W1D 3QY

www.bloomsbury.com

A CIP catalogue record for this book is available from the British Library

ISBN 978 0 7475 9338 6

10 9 8 7 6 5 4 3 2 1

Printed in Great Britain by Clays Ltd, St Ives plc

The paper this book is printed on is certified independently in accordance with the
rules of the FSC. It is ancient-forest friendly. The printer holds chain of custody.

FSC
Mixed Sources
Product group from well-managed
forests and other controlled sources

Cert no. SGS-COC-2061
www.fsc.org
© 1996 Forest Stewardship Council

'The traitor to humanity is the traitor most accursed.'
–James Russell Lowell, *On the Capture of Certain Fugitive Slaves*

chapter one

The blindfold is firmly tied. My consciousness is divided between the darkness that my eyes strive to penetrate and my stark terror. When the blindfold is removed, the first thing I register is the face of the man who is to be my interrogator. He is standing, and I am sitting, but my gaze instinctively seeks out this man's face. It's not an attractive face. I can see immediately that he knows the impact his appearance will have on a young woman — a child, really — snatched from the streets without warning. He knows everything about my terror.

He is tall, fat, and bald, and he stinks. I don't know whether the stink comes from his breath or from his body, but it is foul, like the reek of rotting meat. He is perhaps fifty years old, with an untidy beard streaked with grey. He wears a long shirt hanging out over his trousers.

He draws himself up even more fully erect and stares down at me, as if to reinforce the dominance not only of his stature, but of the power he has over my life. Some part of my mind, even in the midst of my fear, recognises that this man is enjoying himself, and that this is only the beginning of his enjoyment. He has already summed me up: a pampered middle-class princess from the university, playing at politics in street protests against the regime. I'm a toy to him. Maybe he hates me, too, but more important than his hatred is the enjoyment I will provide him with. I am guessing at his opinion of me, of course; the only things I can really be sure of are my fear and my aching desire to be safe, to be in the care of someone — my father, my mother — who wishes me exactly the opposite of what this man has in store for me.

I know where I am, or at least I can guess: this is Evin Prison, in northern Tehran, some kilometres from my home in the inner suburbs. I have heard of this place; everyone I know has heard of it – all of my friends from university. We all know it is a place to be avoided, but only in the way that the good people in children's stories know that they must avoid the ogre's castle. It truly did not occur to me that a good person – me! – could be dragged into this bad place.

What had I done to deserve this? Voiced a few opinions, handed around petitions, gathered in street protests with my friends. I had never hurt anyone, never fired a gun, never thrown a stone. This was the horrifying contradiction of my situation: I wanted it to be known that I was a good person, someone who loved peace and books and conversations with my friends, but this man who stood before me did not care. If he'd been instructed to kill me, he would have killed me. The world he inhabits is brutal, primitive. There is nothing in him to which I can appeal. Nothing whatsoever.

The interrogator lets the reality of my situation sink in. He sits at a desk facing me, and says nothing for some time. Finally, he looks down at some papers spread on his desk. 'Zarah Ghahramani, born in 1981, with birth certificate number 992 issued in Tehran, a student doing a translation course. Is that right?'

'Yes,' I reply softly.

He strikes the table hard with the flat of his hand and I almost leap from my chair, such is my shock. My eyes had been slightly averted, half-closed, but now they are open wide — as wide as they can possibly be.

'When you wanted to change the future of the country at the university, were you speaking so softly?' he shouts.

I don't respond. Just for a split second, I shut my eyes and rapidly pray for God to intervene and make me safe.

The interrogator hits the table once more, as loudly as the first time. I don't move.

'When I ask you something, answer me, do you understand?'

'Yes,' I reply, my voice seeming to come from somewhere far away from where I sit.

The interrogator leans back in his chair and tugs at the strands of his beard.

'What is your name?' he asks, when he is good and ready.

'Zarah Ghahramani,' I reply.

'Full details!' he shouts.

I swallow to free my throat of the constriction of fear.

'Zarah Ghahramani,' I answer, in a voice neither too soft to antagonise this man, nor too loud, for that might make me seem belligerent. I am rapidly trying to educate myself in this man's preferences, trying to learn what expression, what tone of voice, what demeanour will placate him just enough to save me from his temper. 'Born in Tehran, birth certificate number 843, student of translation, entrant of year 1377.'

He makes no response at first. His plump hands are toying with a pen on the table before him. My gaze becomes transfixed by the toying motion of his hands, as if the power he has over me is concentrated in them. I think of what his hands might do to me, not knowing at this moment that those plump hands will become an enduring image in the nightmares that await me, not knowing that what I fear from those hands will come to pass.

I place my own hands on the table. I am making a deliberate attempt to regain some control of myself. I am trying to look like someone who is ready to begin a sensible, logical conversation. Against my better judgement, I am going to treat this dreadful man as if he has some compassion. I am going to speak to him as if he cares about my situation, even though he doesn't. This is whistling in the dark, yes, but I must do something; I must at least try to relieve my humiliation, if only for a few minutes.

He is observing me thoroughly while hiding his stare. When he sees that I have placed my hands on the table, he says, 'Are you ready, then?'

Instantly my courage falters.

'Ready for what?'

He gives me a menacing look.

'Only I ask questions,' he says. 'Do you understand?'

'Yes.'

All of sudden and for no reason he bursts into laughter. His laugh reminds me of the shabby old man in an Iranian novel by Hedayat called *The Blind Bat*. Hedayat says that the shabby old man in the story has a laugh 'that makes your hair stand on end'. If I wasn't so scared, I would sneer at my interrogator for having adopted so many of the clichéd mannerisms of bad guys in books and movies.

'Do you know why you are here?' he says.

I don't answer.

'No,' he replies, answering his own question, 'you don't know, do you? You have to remain here because the country does not need rubbish like you.'

I shake my head as a sign of disagreement. I merely wish to say that I am not rubbish, nor anything like rubbish. Even more foolishly, I say, 'But why?'

He comes abruptly from behind his desk and shoves his face so close to mine that it is almost touching me.

'Didn't I tell you, I am the only one who asks questions!'

I have shut my eyes defensively, as if preparing for a blow. I open them again and feel his spit spraying my cheeks. The foul smell of him! I am close to vomiting, and I would, except that I have not been given anything to eat for days and there is nothing to throw up.

He sits down again and stares across at me with contempt. He waits, letting me dwell in my terror. In God's name, what was I thinking? That this man would talk to me intelligently, reasonably, listen to my side of the story?

He begins to ask me about my family. He speaks in a tone of false intimacy, as if he were an old family friend. How is this person, how is that person? I know perfectly well that he is lulling me into believing that I am now safe, that he has spent his temper and is now going to be calmer, more sensitive. I am waiting for the blow. I know the blow is coming. This vile man with his techniques of interrogation learned from bad movies is aiming his blow, taking his time. How disgusting that he should name the members of my family with his stinking, unwashed mouth! How repulsive that he should use their names! But that is not the blow.

'Tell me,' he says quietly, 'how is the old SAVAKI?'

He means my father.

That is the blow.

chapter two

The interrogator, himself the agent of a tyranny, had invoked the name of an older agency of tyranny. SAVAK had been the state security arm of the Pahlavi regime – the regime that had ruled my country until two years before my birth in 1981. The Shah of Iran, Mohammad Reza Pahlavi, had been swept from power by one of the defining events of the twentieth century, the Islamic Revolution of the Ayatollah Ruhollah Khomeini. SAVAK had been the most detested institution of the Shah, a secret police force licensed to murder, torture, and imprison at will. Even by the hideous standards of such institutions down the centuries, SAVAK stood out as an especially vile example.

SAVAK's agents were known as SAVAKI, but my father had not been one of them. He had been a high-ranking officer in the Shah's army – loyal to Pahlavi, yes, but not a zealot, not a thug, not a killer. The interrogator had wished to shock me by calling my father 'the old SAVAKI'; shock me, sicken me, further reduce my ability to resist his will. He was saying, in effect, 'You are the daughter of a devil, if I say you are. There is no limit to the means I might employ to harm you. Nobody will sympathise with you.'

Although I was born after Khomeini's triumphant return to Iran and grew up under the regime he created, I was raised as if Pahlavi were still in power, or at least as if he might soon return to power. For the first four or five years of my life I was unaware of any rules and restrictions other than those that originated with my mother and father: I ate everything on my plate because there were children starving in other parts of the world; I didn't repeat certain words that my older brothers and sisters sometimes used when angry; and so on. But by 1986, when I turned five, it must have become apparent to my father and mother that the zealots who ruled Iran were there for keeps, and so I was required to adopt a second set of rules and restrictions: an outdoors set imposed by the state.

I became familiar with the protocols of the 'primitives' (a term my father applied to the regime and its supporters) little by little. It was like a gradual initiation into the mysteries of a strange cult. Of course, everyone's childhood is a period of initiation, of trying to comprehend an ever-expanding world. At a certain age, it is thought that a child is ready to have a little more of what is really going on revealed to her or to him, then a little more, and then more still. But children in middle-class homes like mine, born at the same time as me, had to grasp new things that came along in our indoor lives (our 'real' lives, so to speak) while at the same time getting used to outdoor innovations.

The state expected that I would understand things in the way it prescribed; but my family, especially my father, urged on me an alternative way of seeing the world around me. And, on top of this dual understanding, I was expected to keep one way of seeing the world private, only spoken of within the family home, while the second way of being was to engage in a public performance, a way of advertising my loyalty to the state. It was like learning two languages, and remembering when to use one and when to use the other.

In school, I was taught that my greatest loyalty must be to God, then to the father of the Islamic Republic, the Ayatollah Khomeini, and to the nation itself. I was taught about demons as well as about God. Americans were demons. Americans were faithless, perfidious creatures. Americans had been the special friends of another great demon, Pahlavi.

At home, Americans were not such demons, and Pahlavi was spoken of (somewhat apologetically) as a good man misled by the people around him. Freedom and tolerance were valued. A girl was as important as a boy. Love was vital. And Iran, my country, was the captive of sinister, inflexible people who saw the world in black and white, no colour permitted, no shading, no nuances, no tolerance of beauty outside of Islamic spirituality.

It is not so difficult for a child to learn the language and customs and protocols of two worlds in the way that I did. Some children have even greater demands placed on them. But, with the passage of years, the time comes when the child, now a young woman, will wish to speak up more on behalf of one world than another. And that is what happened to me.

—

I turned six in 1987. I had learned the two languages, learned about the two worlds. But there was more to learn, for Iran was at war with Saddam Hussein's Iraq, and had been for the whole of my life. This was a conflict that could not be neatly consigned to one world or the other. Saddam was the man who sent his aeroplanes to bomb Iranian cities; an enemy in each of my worlds, a despised figure in each of my languages. There could be no two ways of thinking about young Iranian men killed in this war; there was nothing ambiguous about death on the battlefield. This conflict contradicted the well-known saying, 'My enemy's enemy is my friend'.

That year, my sixth year, my father, without quite enough forethought, bought me a pair of pink shoes. I adored them the instant I set eyes on them. They were shoes from a fairy story, the enchanted shoes of a princess. I was supposed to wear them on New Year's Day and, according to custom, to walk in them to my grandmother's house and receive my New Year's gift of money. But it was not possible to observe this lovely custom that year. A cousin of my mother, a boy of nineteen, had been killed in the war, and we were in mourning. It is an Iranian tradition that if a family is grieving for the death of a close relative, the family will mourn for a lengthy period of time. As a sign of respect for the soul of the deceased person, we abstain from any activity that creates joy or pleasure. Such traditions of mourning are common all over the world, regardless of religion or culture; but in the Iran of the mullahs, particularly during the war with Iraq, this custom of mourning grew and grew to the point where it ceased to serve a genuine human need and became instead something monstrously neurotic.

For example, the husband of a young woman living next door in Tehran was killed on the battlefield, and this poor woman was expected to forsake smiling at anything from the moment the news reached her for an unknowable number of years into the future – the actual number being dependent on how long the war lasted. Naturally, she had nothing to smile about when she heard of her husband's death, but the proscription on smiling meant that she could not behave in any natural, human way for years to come – she could not even smile at her children. Nor could she even begin to think of courtship until she had served what her family and the state judged to be an acceptable period of widowhood; not that the 'courtship' would have amounted to anything more than an agreement to marry a certain man chosen for her. When the woman was finally permitted to remarry, she remained stigmatised, treated coldly by her own family and the family of her first husband. It was as if everyone but the young woman herself thought that her mourning should be so profound that she would never even think of remarrying. And it was the war, of course, that heightened this madness; it was the war that turned 'martyrdom' into a national fetish.

Within my own family, the war was spoken of as a disaster, pure and simple. My father considered Saddam the aggressor. But the young men who were killed in their tens of thousands, in their hundreds of thousands, were not spoken of as 'martyrs' in the sense that had gained such currency in the Islamic Republic. They were simply the victims of warfare, and it was a sorrow that they should have lost their lives. This was another distinction between the two worlds I inhabited. In the streets, in school, in any public place, the war with Iraq was represented with brazen symbols (such as a salivating Saddam with the horns of a demon), or with words that had the same function as brazen symbols: evil, martyrdom, sacrifice. But my father and mother were intelligent and sophisticated people. They understood the world in more complexity than did many Iranians, as well they might, with the advantage of their education and privileged position in pre-revolutionary Iran.

So the war introduced a further difficulty for me, another

psychological impediment to behaving in a natural and spontaneous way in public, because I wasn't free to think of the war as purely and simply a clash between Good and Evil: the rulers of Iran were in the right in fighting Saddam, but they were not above criticism themselves. It is this complexity of thought that is so hated by dogmatists like the rulers of Iran, or by dogmatists anywhere. They want you to accept a cartoon or caricature version of the world around you, but you can't go along with them. You hate the falseness of it. You want the freedom to think for yourself.

My pink shoes, which I wore now and again after the mourning for my relative had been thoroughly observed, were what I would now call 'slip-ons' – flat soles, no laces or buckles, a bit like ballet shoes. The front of each shoe was ornamented with an artificial flower that was also pink in colour, but a darker pink than the body of the shoe. At the age of seven, those shoes expressed more about the world in which I wanted to live than anything I could possibly have put into words. In a strange way, those pink shoes and my love of them and my appetite for the places I might go in them led me, after many twists and turns, to a cell in Evin Prison.

chapter three

The interrogator takes his cigarettes from the pocket of his trousers. Without haste, he plucks a single cigarette from the packet, strikes a flame from his lighter, and puts it to the tip. I am grateful that he is a smoker. I am more than grateful; I am overjoyed. For while he is involved in the procedure of lighting up, I am given a respite from questions, insinuations, outright accusations, threats, and humiliation.

He knows this, of course. He knows that I am experiencing relief. Whatever I am feeling, at any moment, he knows. He has a job that engages his natural sadism. He has a job in the heaven of sadists. He is a happy man. Perhaps, in some tiny part of his mind, he loves me. Look at what I provide for him! The opportunity to gloat, menace, torture. And what a rewarding subject of sadism I am: terrified out of my mind, staring at him with eyes filled with pleading.

'You don't know what I mean when I say "the old SAVAKI", do you?' he says. I tell him that I don't know what he means, even though I know perfectly well. I am learning about my interrogator even as I sit here. I am learning to say only what he wants to hear. If he wishes to hear anything about my father, about my father's politics, or my father's ambitions for Iran, it will be he who will tell me, not the other way around.

He studies me closely. Perhaps he thinks I am learning the rules a little too quickly. He makes a gesture with his hand – just a small motion, but it is dismissive.

'Don't play with me,' he says, menacingly. 'You are no match for me. Every day, I make people like you talk in this room. Some of them,' he adds, after a pause, 'I send to the next life.'

This is meant to further increase my fear. But, oddly enough, I find myself laughing on the inside, as if my sense of humour demands some expression. I do not laugh aloud. That would be insane. That would end in punishment, or worse. People of this man's sort have no capacity whatsoever for smiling at their melodramatic language, at their own silliness. But, honestly, 'Some I send to the next life'? He sounds like a rotten actor in a cheap soap opera.

The reek of my interrogator's breath wafts across the space between us. It strikes my face like a blow from a fist. I feel my stomach begin to convulse, but I maintain control.

'What is your father up to these days?' my interrogator asks, settling into a new phase of questioning.

'He runs his business,' I reply, which is the simple truth.

'And his friends? His associates? Who are they?'

'I don't know.'

He looks down at the papers on his desk, taking his time.

'You don't know?'

'I don't know.'

He makes some notes on the papers before him. He keeps his hand extended at the top of the sheet of paper he is writing on, to prevent me seeing anything. I recall all those goody-goodies in high school using the same strategy as the interrogator is using to prevent anyone copying their precious answers. What does he think I will discover if I glimpse his stupid notes? That he can't spell? That his handwriting is untidy? Just imagine that I had the courage or the madness to sneak a look at his notes and say, shaking my finger, 'That's not how you spell "Traitor to the Revolution". Now write it out fifty times correctly.'

'You don't know who your father's associates are? Is that what you expect me to believe?'

'Yes.'

He shakes his head in contempt, then repeats his question, and repeats it again, betraying his impatience with gestures of his hand and expressions of disdain. My head is beginning to throb. Why all these questions about my father? What has this to do with me? Is it my father who is the real subject of the interrogation? Am I no more than a pawn? I can't think any longer in any alert way. And inside my head a pleading voice is whispering, *Please let me go, please let me go* ... When my friends and I heard of fellow students being picked up by the police and questioned in a room like this one I sit in now, how brave we were about the way we would behave! As I stare at my interrogator, I recall myself thinking, only weeks earlier, *Why, I will simply tell the truth. I will stand up proudly and shame the fools by refusing to cower, refusing to weep, refusing to tremble.* Silently, I censure myself: *Oh, Zarah, what a child you were! Where is your pride now?*

'Tell me, what does your father think of Khatami?'

'Khatami?' I ask, growing stupid with fatigue. Why is he asking about the nation's prime minister, a man with the reputation of being a liberal, a man he no doubt hates?

'What did your father think about Khatami's election?'

'I don't know.'

'Did he vote for Khatami?'

'I don't know.'

It is likely that this obese man with the foul breath and the melodramatic manner knows exactly who my father voted for in the last national election. I doubt that he asks any questions which he does not already know the answers to. This game is exhausting me. How can I possibly answer? Can I say, 'Oh, since you ask, my father hates the regime that you represent. When he listens to the news on the radio, he rails against the lies and hypocrisy of the mullahs. He believes that you and your masters are squeezing the life out of Iran. He detests your sanctimony, your corruption. And, as a matter of fact, he often compares the Iran of today with the Iran of the Pahlavi years. Maybe the Shah's regime was as vile and corrupt and cruel as you say, but not everyone who served the Shah was a thug. My father is a good man. He would not have sat before a terrified girl and bullied her as you do. And his breath is not like yours, and he would never allow himself to take on your grotesque form.' I can't say anything remotely like this. But how I wish I could!

My first interrogation ends with these exhausting questions about my father. The interrogator gestures to a guard. I am blindfolded once more. The guard nudges me to make me walk. I follow a long route back to my cell.

Dear God, how I love this cell! It is dark and cold and the walls are damp, but I adore it! I sit on the bed and simply enjoy breathing. Then the fear grips me again. They have not finished with me, surely? Will they blindfold me again, take me to that hideous man? Is this only the first of many times that I will sit before him, struggling to learn the rules of his ugly games? I know the answers to these questions that have formed in my poor, weary brain: *the first of many times, Zarah.*

I cannot bear it. I cannot bear it.

chapter four

My sensibility as a child, as I have already suggested, was a pink-shoe sensibility. I loved pretty things like bright red hair-clips and my mother's Kurdish necklaces and bangles. And I loved the under-the-counter Western pop music my sisters bought in the bazaars. This predilection was bound to make trouble for me in a country where a very stern version of Islam had been imposed. The odd thing was that I had no argument with Islam; on the contrary, I admired the beauty of its spirituality, its essential humanity. As an adult, I came to see Islam as a profound expression of the desire of human beings to embrace the divine. But in the Iran I grew up in, respect for Islam, admiration of its philosophical and spiritual core, was not quite enough. One was asked to practise super-piety. If I had grown up in a Calvinist state, in a Puritan state, in a fundamentalist Protestant state, in any state that insisted on a severe expression of belief, I would have faced the same problems.

I was not a frivolous child; but I loved fun, I loved colour, I loved the joy I could find in quite simple things, and I couldn't make myself believe that my salvation depended on following an iron-clad set of rules that had the effect of placing the thrill a. wonder of being alive at such a remote distance from my natural appetites. With the home life I enjoyed, no wonder that the life in the streets — at least that part of it under scrutiny by the mullahs, the police, and the Basiji (the regime's youth militia) — puzzled and perplexed me, even while I made sure that I was not infringing any public rules of dress and conduct.

The predominance of the colour black was at times baffling to me. In the 1980s, the early years of the Islamic Revolution, there were few variations on basic black from the head downwards for Iranian women. Girls below the age of eight were allowed more latitude; but, after a girl's eighth birthday, it was as if a state-appointed sentry had taken up a position outside her front door, ready to cast his gaze over the attire she set forth in each day — attire she discarded with relief when she returned home. The dress code prevented girls like me doing what we yearned to do: sparkle in the sunlight.

Despite my observance of Islamic protocols, I was not, in fact, Muslim. My father was a firm believer in Islam, without being a zealot; but my mother was a Zoroastrian, and she raised me in her faith. She was from Kermanshah in the north-west of Iran, 250 miles from Tehran, a region that for some thousands of years has been the home and sanctuary of Zoroastrians. When I was still very young, no more than five years old, my mother took me to Zoroastrian ceremonies of dedication and worship, where a flame burnt as the symbol of the radiant light that is at the heart of all life in our world, and beyond. I learned to honour the light, to join in the ecstatic dancing that creates a unity of soul and the life-force, and to worship the beauty of all that lives and breathes. Even a child can begin to feel the influence of her soul in her life, as I did, and can begin to understand its vitality.

My father's prayers at home, honouring Allah, had the same purpose. He, too, honoured life and light and the soul. There was never any competition between religions within our household. My father respected my mother's beliefs; my mother respected my father's. My brothers and sisters and I considered it quite normal to live in a household where both Allah and Zoroaster were worshipped – not all that uncommon a state of affairs in Iran, where many Muslims (although not the fundamentalists) harbour a fugitive respect for the more ancient religion.

I was permitted at the age of six to choose the religion I wished to practise, although I must concede that I would have been inclined to uphold my mother's religious observance whatever it may have been, since I was so close to her, and so admired her. Both Zoroastrianism and Islam were conscientiously explained to me. After that, the question was simply: What do you think, Zarah? Which has the greater appeal? My introduction to Zoroastrianism was somewhat in the fashion of Christian children learning about Jesus for the first time. Jesus, for children, is the best of all good guys; gentle, kind, forbearing. Zoroaster was spoken of to the children of his followers in rather this way, even thought he was not a Son of God sent to Earth to redeem us all, but someone who spoke for himself, and for the Light, and against the chaos of the Night. The emphasis was placed on what actually is a profound conviction of the religion, even though it sounds sugary: niceness or, more specifically, nice talking, nice behaviour, nice thinking. I don't feel inclined to elaborate on 'niceness', notwithstanding its shallow connotations to people outside the religion. Zoroastrians simply maintain that it is best to be nice, and that is exactly what I have come to believe.

As a child, I felt utterly at home in the Zoroastrian community. I loved the costumes (which were really versions of ancient Persian national dress: billowing silks of many colours, scarves, and dainty slippers) and the celebrations of seasons. The temperament of the men, women, and children I met at celebrations added to the attraction. There was nothing hard-line about them; nothing dogmatic. Zoroastrianism is not a proselytising religion (and just as well: looking for converts to a religion other than Islam is punishable by death in Iran); its message of reverence for life is not so much broadcast as demonstrated.

My mother would speak to me of the Persia that once was (so far as she knew, of course, and one would have to allow for a certain amount of idealising, since the Persian Empire and its lingering influence has been a thing of the past for a thousand years), and of the persecution that had beset Zoroastrianism since the triumph of the Islamic Revolution. Her complaint, which became my complaint, was that the ancient religion of Persia had been suppressed not by Persians, but by Arabs, and I suppose it can be argued that Islam is foundationally the religion of Arabic peoples.

Is this confusing? Perhaps I should point out that Iranians and Arabs are ethnically distinct peoples, Arabs being a Semitic people whose origins are Middle Eastern, and Iranians an Aryan people who migrated to the Middle East from the subcontinent and from Anatolia about 4000 years ago. The Muslim Arabs overran Iran almost a thousand years ago, and imposed Islam on a people who followed a number of ancient faiths, including Zoroastrianism. I must confess that this particular prejudice of Zoroastrianism has left me with a very Iranian-like disdain for Arabs, a little at odds with my belief in tolerance.

Growing up as I did, I knew that everything was not right when liberties I enjoyed at home vanished the moment I walked out of our front door. A habit of questioning took root in me. Often my questions were voiced: I asked my father and mother why something was as it was. My father's answers were emphatic and political; my mother's were sometimes evasive and always cautionary. Their responses, I now think, were broadly in keeping with those of the female and male parent down the centuries. My mother's priority was to save her children from harm; my father's priority was to highlight injustice. I didn't have a priority – merely puzzlement, sometimes bafflement. But as I grew older and became a student in high school, and then at university, it was my father's indignation that influenced me more than my mother's caution.

chapter five

I am sitting in my cell, petrified with fear. I begin to feel that I may be going mad, or even that I am mad already. How would I know? Who will say to me, 'Zarah, you are perfectly sane. Don't worry about it'?

I sit and stare at the door of the cell, at the slot through which the guard drops my blindfold when it is time for me to be escorted back to the interrogator. I stare at the floor. I stare at my feet. In my mind's eye, I watch myself sitting there, thin and pale and trembling, my shoulders hunched. And this is the girl who poses such a threat to the state?

Even in this pathetic state, my mind is attempting to make sense of my situation, searching for comparisons.

I am a cancer patient. My condition is terminal. I will suffer, then die.

Is this the right metaphor?

Is a better metaphor that of the nightmare? I am dreaming, and the dream is horrifying. Can I force myself awake? Can I discover that I am at home, in my own bedroom? Can I cry out to someone, to my mother? Will she come to my room, full of concern? Will she hug me, murmur endearments? No. I can't wake myself. Whatever evil lurks in my nightmare, it will do with me as it will.

Is this the metaphor I want?

I try out other comparisons, each one dramatising my helplessness. I think of the vastness of this prison, like a city. In each of its thousands of cells a person like me is sitting and struggling to retain some self-respect; or, more likely, like me, struggling not to retain self-respect but to locate the words that will save her or him. What confession would these interrogators like to hear? Because I will confess. I will sign whatever paper is placed before me.

The effort is too great. My mind lapses and drifts.

I find myself listening to a story or, more accurately, watching a story unfold. I am in the story. I am five years old, out shopping with my mother. The war is raging in Iranian cities, particularly in Tehran; it is the mid-1980s. Food shortages leave shelves bare in some stores; at others, people queue for hours to purchase items that are difficult to find, such as vegetables, spices, and cooking oil. It doesn't matter how early you turn up at a store; others have arrived earlier still. Some camp outside stores overnight, with pillows and blankets and a basket of food.

My mother carries a large basket; her free hand has a firm hold of my much smaller hand. She must make sure she doesn't lose her place in the queue. It would be a catastrophe if she were to lose hold of me for a moment, then have to leave her place and find me. The store has only a limited quantity of rice to sell. If my mother misses out, it may be months before a new shipment of rice becomes available. She would have to purchase rice on the black market at ten times the price she can get it for today.

The queue becomes longer and noisier minute by minute. The dawn is just beginning to lighten the sky above Tehran.

People and cars now fill the street. The traffic fumes become more acrid, and the eternal blaring of car horns gathers volume. The women in the queue – and the queue is made up almost entirely of women – chatter like birds. I hear stories of grief; I hear happier stories of a relative returning from the battlefield with all of his limbs intact; I hear complaints of all sorts. I am used to this type of congregation of women, their voices never ceasing as they draw comfort from each other, offer consolation.

My mother is chatting with another woman, talking very softly and at times whispering. My mother is shaking her head in agreement with what the other woman is saying; it is probably some complaint about the government. As they talk, they each keep their eyes on the face of the other. It is intimate, important. 'Yes, yes, I understand what you're saying,' my mother murmurs, nodding her head. I am watching closely, listening closely, fascinated by this parliament of women. The crowd has grown so big that I am being hemmed in, and my grasp on my mother's hand and hers on mine is becoming less secure. Suddenly, there is some disturbance in the queue – perhaps somebody trying to barge through – and, just as a great flock of birds will rise and scatter briefly from fright, so the women of the queue shriek and flutter and become unconnected individuals before once again forming an orderly, communal shape.

But my mother is no longer holding my hand.

I am baffled, then worried, then terrified, all within seconds.

I am lost in the crowd.

I can recognise many faces, but not that of my mother.

I run from woman to woman in my panic, my heart aching with the need to be beside one particular woman.

Rain begins to fall, heavy rain. In seconds, my clothes and shoes are sopping wet.

A voice in my head is telling me that what has happened cannot happen, my mother is somewhere close by, it is not possible for her to lose me, it is not possible for me to be lost.

I picture the face of the woman who was talking to my mother, but I cannot see this face in the crowd either. The rain is now so heavy that my hair is stuck to my head and face; and I am cold, cold, cold. The tip of my nose, my cheeks, and my ears are freezing.

I begin to grow sick with worry about my mother, as well as about myself. When she is panic-stricken, her lips and hands tremble. I imagine how pale she must be, searching for me, how rapidly her heart must be beating. I am beginning to grow more distressed for my mother than for myself now, and I burst into tears and throw my head back and howl my eyes out. Strangers try to comfort me: 'What is the matter, little one? Why so many tears?' But my mother has told me over and over, *Never talk to strangers; go to a policeman if you become lost*. Now, when the strangers try to help me, I cry louder than ever and back away, and the strangers think I am mentally unbalanced and leave me crying.

I wander about hopelessly, brushing against people, looking left and right, and howling, howling, until my voice disappears.

At last, when there is no longer any possibility of such a thing happening, my mother appears before my eyes. Her beautiful face is distorted by grief and fear and the sickness of panic. Her veil is pushed to one side and her black hair falls forward. She grabs me by the shoulders, thrusts my head against her body. I can hear the thud of her heart as I grasp handfuls of her clothing and pull myself closer to her, closer. I want to be her and not a separate person, a separate thing.

She draws my face away and holds it between her hands. Tears run down her cheeks in streams, and yet she is not sobbing. She abruptly slaps me on the face, and it is a hard slap. My face is so numb with the cold that I barely feel a thing, only hear the sound. 'Didn't I tell you not to leave my side? Didn't I say that to you, Zarah? If you are lost once more, I will die. Do you want me to die? Do you want me dead?'

This warning sets me off howling again. 'In the name of God, don't die!' I plead. 'If you die, my friends will have mothers, but I won't!'

My mother relents. She is still trembling, but there is a painful joy in her eyes. She presses my hand, knits her fingers between mine. 'Promise me you will never become lost again,' she says. 'Promise me, Zarah.'

I promise.

In my cell, I cover my face with my hands.

I promise.

chapter six

My mother's cousin was killed in the war against Iraq when he was not much older than a kid. The death grieved my mother terribly. I would catch her sobbing as she combed her hair in the mirror. If she noticed me watching, she would smile and pretend that everything was okay. 'I'm fine, sweetheart. It's nothing.' Mum had a brother fighting in the war, and I felt sure that she was thinking both of him and of her cousin when tears ran down her cheeks. She kept the radio on all day long, and would pace up and down anxiously while she listened to the news.

The war was everywhere. You didn't have to listen to the radio to know that something frightful was going on. Pictures of 'martyrs' were shown on the television – young men with unsmiling expressions, some looking scared, some full of bravado. These pictures would have been taken when those young men first joined the army. Not every young man who died in battle appeared on the television, of course; often, more died in a day than could possibly be displayed on the screen.

I saw widows in the street, so many. Even without any insignia, I knew when a woman had lost a son or a husband just by her face. Iranians feel grief very deeply, regardless of religion. Grief has its roots deep in our Persian past. The depth of our grieving has to do with the importance of love in Iranian culture. This may sound very strange to those Westerners who have been encouraged to adopt a cartoon-like version of Iranians – suicide bombers, war-mongers, religious zealots. But love is the more important thing to grasp when you study Iranians. And this has been true even in Persia's Islamic period. If Westerners would look more closely at our national poets, they would develop a more accurate and more just comprehension of the Persian sensibility. My mother's grief for her young cousin was not simply dutiful or even conventional. She loved her cousin. She loved everyone in her family. And a death in the family was a catastrophe.

The war was all around us, too, when we visited my mother's family in Kermanshah, and my father's family; both of my parents were Kermanshahis. The city is only one hundred kilometres from the Iran–Iraq border in the west of Iran. This is the region of Iran where the majority of Iranian Kurds live, and also the region where Zoroastrianism has its most committed adherents. In many ways, Kermanshah is more Persia than Iran. It is still easy to imagine, in Kermanshah, the ancient kingdom of perfumed gardens, nightingales, sherbert, the music of the dulcimer. Well, it is easy to conjure this Persian past in peacetime, at least. During the war, it was hellish. The city lay in reach of Iraqi bombers, and it was an inviting target with the oilfields and refineries nearby. When we visited one summer during the middle years of the war, the Iraqis bombed the refineries. I heard the thud of the bombs exploding and the screams of the people in the streets. Fires turned the horizon a vivid orange-red. The refineries burned like a furnace for a week and it rained oil. The oil did not come down like the rain in a storm; it drizzled. Tiny droplets formed a coating on everything. The air stunk.

In the streets of Kermanshah and Tehran (and this would surely have been true for every other Iranian city, every Iranian town), I saw war widows scrounging for food for their children, desperate to keep their kids alive. In spite of the government's incessant lauding of the 'heroes and martyrs' of the war, the widows of those martyrs usually struggled for life with the breadwinner gone. The welfare infrastructure in Western nations that supports those who cannot get by or who have met with misfortune did not exist in Iran – or not in any evolved way. Often the widows became beggars, or relied on the charity of relatives. Iranian families are close-knit and supportive, but in many families the help they could offer was limited by poverty. The plight of orphans was even worse. The Kermanshah bombing created hundreds of new orphans in a single night.

I saw fathers who came back from war to find nothing. House, wife, children – all blown to smithereens. Prisoners of war sometimes found no trace of the life they had lived years before. In some ways, even more heartbreaking was the experience of POWs who returned after years of captivity, only to discover that they had been listed not as POWs but as having been killed. I knew of and saw such men, who had been carried off to war on a wave of patriotism, praised for their dedication to the nation and to the ideals of the Revolution. They found that their widows had remarried, often out of dire necessity, and that they were not welcome; they were an embarrassment.

Everyone in Iran, my family included, became bleakly familiar with returnees from the war whose minds were so jolted and wrenched by their experiences that they could never again regain their sense of belonging to anyone or anything. The experience of these wretched men in certain ways mirrored those of Vietnam veterans in America and Australia. It was as if they had stared into an abyss and seen things so horrifying that the morality and dogma that underpinned the society they had been fighting to protect seemed ridiculous, pitiable. One of my older relatives fought for the entire eight years of the war and, over that period, became a complete stranger to the rest of us in his family. He took leave very infrequently: only six times in those eight years. He didn't like taking leave; only injury or the insistence of senior officers (and he was quite senior himself, and highly decorated) would force him to leave the front. Fighting the war meant more to him than anything else in life. He was, I suppose, a born warrior.

When the war ended, he could no longer avoid facing the other part of his life – the domestic part, the part that he was unable to commit himself to, being a warrior. He returned to find his eldest son in an appalling state: addicted to heroin, half-crazed, ill, his face haggard and his expression haunted. We didn't know how to talk to the son or to the father. My uncle attempted to gloss over the tragedy, to pretend that both the father and son were okay; it was just his way of trying to bring both of them back into the embrace of the family. He said to the father, the war hero: 'Is this the son that you have raised? He does not come to visit us and he is always spending time with his friends and having fun.' The father responded with a bitter smile: 'When we were at war defending you and your dignity, we expected that all of you back here would look after the well-being of our families. We returned to you your land and honour intact. Your trust in us was fulfilled. But what of our trust in you?'

Will I sound precocious if I say that the war wearied me, left me exhausted? Will it sound egocentric to the reader if I say that the war blighted my childhood, forced me to mature too quickly? After all, the young men at the front who were compelled to clear minefields by marching over them, who experienced the horror of gas attacks, bombardments that went on for days at a time, who fought in a half-starved state, who were sacrificed in suicidal attacks over open ground – these Iranians and their families surely have the most to complain about. And that is true. But war creates casualties both on and off the battlefield. Iranian children of my generation became secondary victims of war. We all grew up without knowing the joy of being children. Our smiles were guilty smiles. Our laughter was thought obscene. Our daydreams were censured as irresponsible. The unyielding severity of the regime's dogma was further intensified by war propaganda. The little niches in which Iranian children might have expressed their natural exuberance were all shut down, filled in, closed off. What the regime's brand of piety did not destroy, the misery of war suffocated. Children of seven and eight wore the expressions of adults.

That period of my life – the period of my fugitive childhood – left me with a longing to create a proper childhood for my own children, when those children come along, as I hope with all my heart they will. May they never feel inclined to wear black, those children that I so crave. May they keep their faces exposed to the world all day long. May they only ever think of aeroplanes as friendly machines that carry people to other cities, other countries, and that never drop high explosives on neighborhoods full of terrified people. The stories I read to my children will not be stories of martyrs. The rules I lay down for them will have nothing to with sacrifices, nothing to do with an afterlife; the rules will only insist on courtesy, tolerance. Their obligations will be to find happiness, and to preserve it. When I breast-feed my baby, I hope I can do so without listening for the sound of the Red Alert siren, waiting for a catastrophe brewed up by men mad with ego. Above all, may my children never be required to comprehend things beyond their age. May they never know without being told that the woman over there with the pale, anxious face has just heard that her husband has become a martyr.

chapter seven

I can keep a very imperfect track of the time by listening to the call of the muezzin over the prison's PA system. I know, or think I know, that it is now a little past midnight. I'm being prodded and pushed down the corridor by the guard. Interrogations go on around the clock in Evin. The interrogators work in shifts, only stopping to pray.

I am blindfolded. The guard forces me down onto a chair in what I think is the same interrogation room I've been taken to before. I expect the blindfold to be removed, as it has been at each interrogation up until now. But the blindfold is not removed.

I try to see my surroundings in my mind's eye. I know the bare wooden table is just in front of me. High on the wall above the desk is a long, horizontal window, blacked out with paint and tape. The door to the right is a heavy thing, made of metal, meant to deter any idea of a sudden rush for freedom. The walls are painted a drab grey, scratched up to the height that a man's arms might reach. I can easily imagine how those scratches came to be there.

I hear footsteps approaching, and I feel sure that the footsteps are not those of the fat man. How I can be so sure, I don't know;

I had not intentionally memorised the sound of the fat man's footsteps. I can hear with startling clarity the sounds of this new man's movements as he stalks about the room. Without wishing to, I turn my head this way and that in an attempt to follow his movements. This is obviously a reflex: the need to seek out the enemy with one's vision, even when one's eyes are bound. I have the sense that the interrogator's movements are designed to torment me. I feel certain that it amuses him to watch me groping for him in such a futile way.

It's so easy to imagine all of these torturers, everywhere in the world, getting their start in their chosen profession by teasing animals, plucking the wings off flies, drowning kittens in bathtubs. As adults, they retain all the worst features of repellent little boys, exercising power over the powerless. Even as I struggle with the fear that this new interrogator's tactics arouse in me, I make a crazy mental note to ridicule him for his infantile sense of humour at some time in the future, when I am free.

The movements stop behind the chair I'm sitting in. My hearing has developed such hypersensitivity that I can hear this man's breathing as if it were amplified, even though it is not wheezy or laboured.

'How did you come to know Arash Hazrati?' the interrogator asks.

This is a different voice, a softer voice. Absurdly, I find myself thinking, *Oh, I hope he's nice!* Why do I entertain such a hope? Because his voice is soft? Oh, it's idiotic, but I can't help it! I so need this miracle, that the new man will turn out to be a nice man! I make a promise to him in my head: *If you are nice, I will never ridicule you, never!*

He's waiting for my answer, just as I was waiting for this question.

Arash is the leader of the protests at the university, and he's my friend. He's a teacher, not a student. He's been arrested a number of times, brought here to Evin and kept here for months at a time. Sometimes when I meet him and ask how he is, he grins and says, 'Missing Evin.' He never spoke in detail about what he'd endured, so it is only now that I understand how brave he was to be able to make such a joke. He was studying law last year, but they wouldn't let him finish his degree. Everybody loves Arash – everybody that I love, at least. Arash is a hero, a lion, and the regime loathes him.

I'm still entertaining my childish hope that this new man, this new interrogator, will be a nice interrogator, caring and gentle and well-mannered, a gentleman, a knight.

Instead of answering his question, I ask if I can remove my blindfold.

'No,' he says quietly. 'Just listen to my questions and answer them very carefully. If you don't answer my questions carefully, I will get angry. Do you want me to get angry?'

My dream of being treated nicely by a nice man dissolves in an instant, as it was bound to, as I knew it would.

'I only knew him through university,' I answer, hoping that this is what he means by answering carefully. 'We study at the same university.'

'Is that all?' the new interrogator asks.

'Yes.'

He commences reading a list of times and dates. On these dates, at these times, Arash and I have been seen together. He wants to know what Arash and I were doing at these times, on these dates. But I can't remember. And how does the interrogator know all this stuff? Are all the times and dates true? I make a decision that causes an alarm to go off in my head, a warning bell. I am going to deny that I have seen Arash at the times I am said to have seen him, on the dates I am said to have seen him. I am going to deny every single one. What can these people prove? They can prove nothing. I will deny and deny and deny.

'I only know him a bit, and always see him on campus, and that's it,' I answer.

The interrogator laughs. It is not a loud, bellowing laugh. 'Well, it appears that you think I'm an idiot,' he says. 'Listen to me. I'm going to leave you alone here and you are going to have a look at some photos I will leave in front of you. Study them very carefully. Write down anything that you remember about them. Anything at all. Understood?'

I hear the interrogator leave the room. I hear the door open and close. I hear his footfalls in the corridor.

Tentatively, I remove the blindfold.

It's the same room as last time.

I am seated quite close to the wooden table. A number of photos are laid out on it. They are coloured photos, each one about twenty centimetres by fifteen. The photos each show me and Arash together, sometimes with other friends. There are close-ups, full-length shots, and shots obviously taken from a distance with a telephoto lens. Seeing my face in close-up, my smiling face, my laughing face, I feel violated. I have been photographed by a complete stranger at a time when I was happy and carefree. Whoever took these pictures had no right to do so. The intimacy in the pictures belongs to me, to Arash, and to my friends. It's as if the intimacy has been stolen from me.

What a foolish way of thinking! I'm still judging these people — these regime people, these interrogators, these torturers — as if they belong in the same moral and ethical category as normal people. I can't seem to make it stick inside my head that they are not the same: they are above the law; they are not required to account for such things as spying, eavesdropping, taking unauthorised pictures, blindfolding people, beating them, humiliating them. Why can't I make it stick? Why am I shocked at each new violation? Is it because I believe what the constitution of Iran says about the rights of its citizens? That no citizen can be snatched from the street, locked up, denied legal representation, compelled to make confessions? Because that is exactly what my country's constitution guarantees — freedom from arbitrary arrest and coercion. Even though I've been told of countless cases of people who oppose the government being locked up and abused, I haven't been able to make myself accept that those people who serve the government of my country will do me whatever harm they wish.

Here's a picture of Arash and me drinking coffee at a café. Here we are at a rally: Arash, the lion, addressing the crowd, his arm raised, and me, on the platform gazing at him adoringly. And — dear God! — here I am going into Arash's house! And here I am leaving the house a few hours later, according to the notation of time and date on the picture. *How dare they!* I whisper. *How dare they!*

I can explain nothing. Can I tell the interrogator what I was really doing? Impossible. I struggle to make the pen work, struggle to write.

I write a couple of lines about two of the pictures. That's all.

I hear a knock on the door of the cell.

I replace the blindfold.

The interrogator enters the room. I hear him pick up the sheet of paper on which I have written so little.

'So, you have forgotten how to write? Yes?'

He hits me hard across the face, with an open-handed slap.

I am shocked. In my whole life, I have never been struck in this way. My mother spanked me; but this is a cold-blooded slap with contempt behind it, not love.

'Listen to me,' says the interrogator, quietly and deliberately. 'I'm going to leave the room again, and I want this paper to be full when I come back. Are your ears open?'

I hear him leaving. I remove the blindfold again, my face still stinging.

I must write something. I must write something. I must. What can I say? What does this man want to hear?

Picture 2. *I had gone to Arash's place to have a look at his library.*

Picture 3. *Me and Arash going to the magazine office to see a friend.*

That's it. I can't write anything else. I don't know what to say. I know that what I've provided will not satisfy the interrogator, but I simply can't think of anything more. I wish I could. I realise that I could write down the names of all my friends who appear in the pictures, but I am very reluctant to do that. My friends could end up in here with me.

I place the pen on the table next to the pictures and the sheet of paper on which I've written. The paper is not full. It's not half-full, not a quarter-full. I replace the blindfold, as I'm compelled to do.

The interrogator hasn't returned. What is he doing? Listening outside the door? Or is he interrogating someone else at the same time as he interrogates me? Is he like one of those chess players who can conduct two or three or four games at once, skipping from board to board, moving a knight, a pawn, a king, always keeping control of the game?

So I wait with my eyes blindfolded.

He's coming. I can hear his footfalls in the corridor. He's opening the door. I can hear his breathing. I imagine him deliberating over what I've written. What he thinks of it, I have no idea. He's laughing, once again not loudly: a short, private laugh. I can hear him doing something, but I have no idea what it is.

Without warning, he hits me – not with his hand this time, but with something else, a belt of some sort. The pain runs up the length of my bare right arm, a frightening pain like an explosion in my skin. The belt is barbed; I am conscious even in the midst of the pain of my flesh being penetrated.

'Why did you do that?' I scream.

I can feel blood flowing.

He hits me again, this time on my right shoulder. The pain is worse than the first time. I fall off the chair to the floor, squirming, thrashing.

'Please don't do this! Please! I wrote about the photos! What else do you want?'

He wrenches me to my feet by my injured arm. The pain is made worse by his grasp, and I scream louder than I have at any time in my life.

He forces me down onto the chair.

'Have I helped you to remember more details?' he says. 'I'm leaving the room. This will be your last chance. When I come back, that paper will be full. If it's not, if you still can't remember, you know exactly what will happen.'

He slaps me on the shoulder where the belt has torn my skin, then leaves the room.

I lift my arm to remove the blindfold, wincing and bleating. The flesh is torn on my right arm. The bleeding puncture-marks are small but they feel deep, as if I'd been stabbed repeatedly with a steel pin. I take up the ballpoint pen in my right hand. The pain in my arm and shoulder is the worst pain I have ever had to cope with, but even stronger than the pain is my devout wish to avoid it being re-administered. It frightens me to think what I would do to avoid being hit again.

What can I write? I can't say what I did at Arash's house, can I? No, I can't. I don't know what the interrogator's response would be. He already considers me depraved for having gone alone to the house of a man who is not my husband. If I tell him what happened, he may use it against Arash. Or he may use it against me.

I sit squeezing the pen, struggling to find a solution to the dilemma. Each second of delay in writing something down carries me closer to punishment. I think I know what I am going to do, but I can't accept that I really will do such a thing. I touch my shoulder where the belt struck me, and flinch. I wait a few seconds, then touch my shoulder again. I whisper to myself, *Coward! Coward!*

This is what I do, finally: I name my friends. I say who each friend is in the pictures.

The guilt makes me wretched, but my moral misery is immediately attacked by self-serving rationalisations: *My friends would do the same if they were sitting here. I'm not a hero. They can't expect me to die for them. They wouldn't die for me.*

And this, above all: *I cannot endure any more. I cannot. I cannot. I cannot.*

I'm crying. My face is wet. But, at the same time, I'm writing. I'm filling the page.

'This is better, isn't it?' the interrogator says when he returns, having given me time to replace the blindfold.

I don't answer. I'm still crying. These are the tears you weep when you discover that your fear of pain is stronger than your convictions. These are the tears you cry when you hate yourself.

39

Dear God, I'd always believed I'd be so much stronger, that I'd resist and resist until death, if needs be. But it's not true. It's not true. I am not the person I hoped I would be.

'Did you have a sexual relationship with Arash Hazrati while you were at his place?' the interrogator asks in his falsely reasonable manner. An answer of 'Yes' to this question, as I understood fully when I refused to give any details of my visit to Arash's house, would likely be followed by a death sentence, and not just my death sentence. The prey they are really stalking is Arash. I am nothing.

'No, never, we were only friends.'

'Why did you go to his house?'

'I wanted to have a look at his library. He has books that I have been looking for, but couldn't find anywhere else.'

'And only he has those books? Yes?'

I see the mistake I've made. I've implicated Arash in the crime of possessing illegal books. I try to extricate myself, and Arash.

'No, I mean he has these really old books …'

'Very good books? Very good books that are illegal, yes? Is that why you went there? Or maybe you wanted to have some fun with your superhero, lying on his bed and reading one of his books? Yes?'

He has his face close to mine. He is holding my chin between his fingers. He is trying to prevent me turning my face away from him.

'Get off me!' I shriek.

'Sorry that my hands are not as soft as his.' He laughs softly at his wonderful wit.

'Did you know you are showing contempt for Islam by entering a house with a male who is not related to you?' he says, sounding very like a clerical magistrate all of a sudden. 'That would be very, very serious.'

What I want to say is that it is also illegal for him to touch me. I want to hiss at him that these rules only seem to apply when it suits him. But I don't say that at all. What I say is this: 'Yes, but I said I only went there to have a look at his library, and it's obvious even from the pictures that I'm holding books when I'm leaving his house. I didn't even take my scarf off.' Then, surprising myself, I add: 'And according to the rules, you shouldn't be touching me, either.'

He slaps me across the face.

'Little girl,' he growls, losing his composure for the first time, 'you don't tell me the rules. I make rules for this place we are in and, if I like, I break them. I can do anything I wish. Do you at last understand?'

I feel strangely happy to have made this disgusting man angry. But immediately I begin to fear that he will wish to make a point – wish to demonstrate his complete power over me, over everyone who is dragged into this cell. I can hear him panting like a dog. He is exaggerating the sound, to alarm me or to amuse himself.

He walks around my chair, stops, waits, then begins to caress my neck with his fingers. He attempts to go further and I struggle to prevent him. I'm screaming, with no regard at all to what further trouble this might land me in. I don't care. Somewhere in the hideousness of this struggle I realise that this pitiable man is actually trying to make me feel his appeal. It's inconceivable, but I truly believe that for him this is some insane form of violent courtship. He's kissing my neck, slobbering over my throat, squeezing my hand. Now I'm begging him to stop, the most earnest begging I can convey. It doesn't stop him. And then I vomit. It heaves up from my stomach with great force and spills down my prison garment.

He steps away from me. 'Bitch!' he says.

I am spluttering and crying at the one time now. The interrogator leaves the room rapidly. Someone else hurries in and grabs my arm, and drags me out and down the corridor. I'm shoved into my cell. The door is pushed shut behind me.

I tear off the blindfold and drop it through the slot. Then, with my eyes liberated, I collapse on the floor, and howl and howl. At intervals I smell the stench of my vomit and the different, sweeter smell of my blood.

chapter eight

Iranians fall in love in exactly the same way as everyone else in the world. Muslims fall in love in the same way as everyone else in the world. Young women in vestments that reach from the crown of their head to their toes fall in love in the same way, by the same process, roused by the same emotions, as young women all over the world.

The liberty to explore a dozen relationships before making a commitment to one man, to one woman, is not available to most Iranians; but this particular liberty, unlike certain others, is perhaps no great loss. In the end, a reasonable compatibility of soul and soul is all that is needed. After that, or so I imagine, it is all a matter of what one has inside: a capacity for loyalty; a desire for affection; spiritual ambition.

I was nearing the end of my first year at Tehran University when I fell in love with one of the very few students who wore a suit on campus. I had noticed him a few times while my girlfriends and I were strolling about the campus in our lunch-break, paying close attention to boys in the way that young women do in Iran: minute observation, but no robust public expression of the interest or delight that we might be feeling.

The way we talked together about boys and sex and good looks and male charisma and desire and longing can be summed up in the Farsi term, *maskhare bazi*. A rough equivalent in English would be 'teasing', but the term suggests something more specific: 'teasing about something that at another time would be taken seriously' perhaps conveys the fuller meaning of *maskhare bazi*.

The man I had noticed was, as the cliché goes, tall, dark, and handsome; but, more importantly, he had an air of quiet self-possession and he projected a maturity beyond his years. (I took him to be in his mid-twenties.) I asked my friends if they knew who he was. Their response was thirty seconds of complete silence. Then came the lecture: I was not to think about him any further; I was to look for someone my own age; I was to come to my senses. The problem was that the handsome man in the business suit with the gentle manner and kind eyes was the eldest son of a very wealthy family. And he and his family were very close to the regime. So his age, his wealth, and his politics should definitely have ruled him out. But I allowed myself to fantasise. I still worshipped Arash, but I could never think of him as my boyfriend; he lived a life aloof from mere boy–girl relationships.

Both my friends and I had the same casual and unfocused complaints about the regime. Irritation and occasional exasperation with the rigid dress code, with the hidebound ideology of the mullahs, with all the do's and don'ts that we were expected to internalise – this made up the substance of our 'opposition' to the regime. Not one of us had developed a sophisticated way of looking at the regime's foundational philosophy; not one of us could have mounted a coherent argument to back up our complaints. The young women in my group of friends could have summed up their politics by saying aloud, 'Hey, girls just want to have fun, okay?'

At the same time, we'd known for years who the enemy was, and during that first year of university our disdain for the regime and its supporters – people like this beautiful man I'd just noticed – had become more specific. Hypocrisy became a special hatred of ours – the hypocrisy of a government that awarded all sorts of treats to the people who endorsed its ideology, whether or not the endorsement was sincere, and withheld favours from those who voiced even the mildest criticism of those in power. Even those who said nothing (because they had nothing good to say about the government) were denied advancement in their careers, better-quality housing, visas to travel abroad, and government contracts.

My friends and I came to see that it was necessary to perjure your soul to earn your share of the favours the government dispensed. Anyone with real money to spend in Iran – I mean big money, what would amount to millions in US dollars – was a friend of the government, by definition. He was not, in most cases, a companion in philosophical outlook, but a means-to-an-end friend. And the man in the smart suit I was eyeing off was, so it was said – by Arash, most importantly, and by those who knew – right up there amongst the country's most accomplished brown-nosing hypocrites.

My infatuation with Behnam found its initial expression in diary confessions. Not long after learning his name and a certain amount about his family and circumstances, I composed a version of a women's magazine 'Is He the Right Guy For You?' checklist:

Me

1. Cute, maybe pretty
2. Down to earth
3. Nineteen years old
4. Well-to-do family, but not rich
5. Mum: easy-going about religion
6. Dad: strong, dependable, a real father, religious up to a point
7. Five siblings
8. Love sport
9. Live in a beautiful suburb, oldest in Tehran, lots of culture
10. Maybe clever, if going to uni means being clever
11. Know nothing about business
12. Don't have my own car

Him

1. Handsome!
2. Arrogant or shy, not sure which
3. Twenty-three years old
4. Admired
5. Mother: very religious
6. Father: businessman living in America
7. Only one brother
8. Not really into sport
9. Lives in the richest suburb
10. Clever, according to the same standard as me
11. Businessman, sort of
12. Has been seen driving at least ten different cars!

The outcome of this highly scientific analysis was 100 per cent negative: we were not exactly born for each other. But in the way that all girls respond when an analysis like this (or an astrological reading, or even plain common sense) contradicts their hopes, I dismissed the outcome. Next day I felt a bit self-conscious telling my friends that I was crazy about Behnam, since they had already explained to me, so kindly, that I was chalk while he was cheese ... and, well, face it, kid, you don't even own a car. (How could I have? The sort of ultra-safe car that my father would have allowed me to drive — a brand-new Volvo, maybe — would've cost an absolute fortune in Iran.) In short, they told me that I was insane. They also said, as a way of compensating me, that he wasn't worth the effort, being so stuck-up.

Behnam walked past me in the corridors of the university without responding in the slightest to my tentative smiles. It was rare for me to see him without a mobile phone at his ear, so my opportunities for letting him know of my existence were extremely limited. Seizing the initiative, I asked a friend, Miriam, who was seeing a friend of Behnam's to introduce me, and so she did. Behnam responded to the introduction as if he were a diplomat of illustrious standing greeting a minor official from some unimportant foreign state. He was formal, correct, politely dismissive. Instead of feeling put-out, I found myself admiring his manners. How courteously he had demonstrated his complete lack of interest in me! Only a true gentleman knows how to do that. And so my infatuation deepened.

Courtships in Iran follow a format that predates the Islamic Revolution, although the mullahs certainly added more tension and more inanity to an already tense and inane ritual. A young woman is permitted to go out with a young man, but only when suitably chaperoned. One chaperone is rarely adequate; a small crowd of the young woman's friends will meet up with a second small crowd of the young man's friends, and the mingled group will watch a movie together, or drink fruit juice, or simply sit down somewhere and smile vacuously. In the midst of all this elaborately choreographed silliness, the relationship of the young man and the young woman is somehow advanced. As unlikely as it sounds, the impediments to intimacy actually enhance one's receptivity – in something of the way, maybe, that the blind often develop extraordinary sensitivity of hearing. One very brief glance from the young man might provide the eloquence of a hundred love poems. Agreement over the choice of a fruit juice might stand for agreement on everything, stretching years into the future. In an odd way, the essence of romance is often better preserved by constraints than by licence.

I became part of my friend Miriam's courtship retinue; Behnam, at the same time, was dutifully helping to make up the numbers in his friend's retinue. The females and males of each retinue took the opportunity (as was expected, and sanctioned) to chat with each other; a form of mass wooing, everybody keeping an eye on everybody else. I tried to chat with Behnam, but was usually too tongue-tied to say anything more engaging than, 'Wow! Hot weather we're having lately, don't you agree?' or, 'Thank you for asking, I am perfectly well.' After a number of these awkward exchanges, Behnam wondered aloud why I was so unforthcoming when I spoke with him. We were sitting side-by-side in the movies. What we were watching, I can't recall, but it would have been something bland and silly that had pleased the government's censors; the wonderful movies made by Iran's small crop of world-class film-makers were only ever shown in secret sessions in garages.

'Why are you so quiet and remote when it comes to me?' he asked in a whisper, and without looking at me.

Such a question is loaded with a disguised intimacy, and is

way outside the rules of the wooing ritual, which do not endorse any question the answer to which would require the employment of a compound sentence. I thought I was about to have a heart attack.

'Maybe because I don't have anything to talk about with you,' I said.

As soon as I spoke, I felt like slapping myself across the face. It sounded so pointedly rude! What on earth was in my head? Because what I really wanted to say was, 'I would love to talk with you freely and naturally. I am besotted with you. I worship the ground you walk on.' Instead of that, I constructed a wall of ice between us. I had to ask myself, 'Zarah, are you the most stupid girl in Tehran, in Iran, in the world? I despair of you!'

Behnam excused himself and shuffled his way past the knees of my friends and his friends. I thought he was going for good. I looked around at my friends, all of them chatting cheerfully, eating popcorn, negotiating the twists and turns of courtship with poise and grace. Why on earth couldn't I be like that?

Underlying the features of courtship local to my own country, the age-old elements of boy–girl relationships, common to all cultures, still endure. Once again, I was attempting to talk two languages – just as I did when, as a child, I had taught myself to speak the language of the Islamic Revolution and the far more fluent language of indoor life. But that was years ago. Now I found it so difficult to pick up this new, circumlocutory language of courtship. That was what made me envious of my friends. I sat there brooding on my self-consciouness, or whatever it was that prevented me from saying in a natural way the sweet or clever or devious or coy things my friends said to the boys they wanted to encourage.

Behnam came back. He had fruit juices for each of us. I

somehow managed to give him a smile — such a simple thing, and yet, for me, so hard! We didn't say a word for the rest of the movie.

I had fallen in love with someone I couldn't even talk to. After that agonising evening at the movies, Behnam and I saw each other now and again, but I stayed away whenever I could without seeming rude because I was terrified of being rejected. He remained courteous and considerate, always enquiring if he could give me a lift to one party or another, but I usually declined. Wretched and fed-up with myself, I finally decided to talk to my Mum about Behnam. I knew that she would listen sympathetically and have something sensible to say — something intelligent, free of dogma. My mother's advice was direct: next time I was asked to a party by Behnam, I should say yes. My mother assured me that Behnam would be getting the better deal: that I was a beautiful girl, that any man would bless the day I came into his life, and so on. Of course, one talks to one's mother in order to be reassured in this way, to be flattered, to have one's self-confidence restored, and that was the effect of my mother's advice on me.

It is customary in Iran to find some roundabout way of asking a girl out. Behnam didn't invite me to parties; he would ask me if I needed a lift. The next time he asked me that question, I said, 'Sure, if it's not out of your way.' The evening unfolded in the manner of a scene in a paperback romance, I am happy to report; I would have no complaints if the whole of life, for everyone, imitated a paperback romance. Everything was perfect: me, him, a beautiful Tehran night, music, the stars.

On the way home, Behnam parked the car in a quiet street in the north of the city, with the stark Alborz mountains rearing above us like huge cardboard cutouts. Even at that late hour of the night, the racket of the city was still audible. Tehran is a machine that throbs along dully after midnight, then rouses to an ear-splitting cacophony in the morning. I love the idling sound of late-night traffic from the city. I love the shouting and arguing and cursing and honking of the daytime, too, but the night-time has its own special allure. I was perfectly well aware that Behnam wanted to kiss me, and I'm ashamed to say that I was not above engaging in that girly, teasing thing of making the man wait a little longer, enjoying the power of it, knowing with certainty that I could ask Behnam to run barefoot around the block if I wanted to, and that he would sigh and complain, but obey.

'Listen to the rumble,' I said. 'It never stops. No, not ever. Don't you love it?'

In my own sweet time, we kissed.

I fell hopelessly in love or, I should say, more hopelessly in love than ever. Behnam's tenderness, his attentiveness to my moods, his courtesy and consideration made me feel as if we two were the most important, and certainly the most glorious, thing happening on earth; that we were a milestone event in the life of the universe. And then along came politics.

I must explain that the business culture of Iran under the mullahs creates mutants: people who have two heads. Businessmen are, by their nature, pragmatists; their gaze is not set on some undefined shape away in the distance, but on a very strongly defined shape not that far away at all. They deal in the concrete. They may not always be hostile to poetry, but they are not themselves poets. And this, I think, is true of the business mentality all over the world. But businessmen may also be sympathetic to the things that poets and visionaries clamour for, such as liberty and justice. In Iran, you can't do business without the support of the regime, in one form or another – including the tacit – and you will not get any support from the regime if you are openly sympathetic to poets and visionaries. So you hide your sympathies, as Behnam did. You never say a word to contradict the policies of the mullahs. But the danger is that you will become what you do; that your silent sympathies will wither for lack of expression and that, even though you continue to whisper your qualified approval of the kids in the streets crying out for change, your heart, your mind, and your soul are the captives of the mullahs.

Behnam was, first and foremost, a businessman: a business pragmatist. He and his father managed a very profitable petrochemical company. His father handled the American end; Behnam, the Iranian end. He was a trusted member of what is known as 'the community' – the corps of Iranian businessmen sanctioned by the regime to maintain the nation's involvement in the world economy. Those in the community are on permanent probation. The unspoken understanding is that, while the members of the business community will not be required to trumpet the regime's ideology, nor will they ever voice any criticism. It is a bit like the tacit agreement that informs some marriages, particularly celebrity marriages: fidelity is not an expectation, but any messing around must be done in secret; it must never reach the front pages.

—

Although I was aware that my politics didn't meet with Behnam's complete approval, I didn't make much of it. After all, Behnam barely had time for politics; he was so busy making deals and trouble-shooting on his mobile phone that it was a wonder he could find time to even notice what was going on in the wider world. But what I didn't realise was that Behnam, for his part, didn't consider that my politics amounted to much; he didn't believe that I had made much of an emotional investment in the things I said I believed in. It was therefore a terrific shock to him when he heard of a speech on reform I'd made before fellow students at the university. He was outraged. When he found me walking down a corridor at the university, he pulled me into an empty classroom.

'What in God's name have you done? Are you insane?'

'I made a speech. I said what I believe. Is that a problem?'

'You know that I'm in the community. You know exactly what I do. You knew it even before we became close.'

'Is it necessary to shout at me?'

'Zarah, what in the hell is going on in your head?'

'Would you please tell me why you think it necessary to scream at me?'

'That's the last time, and I mean the last time, you do such a stupid thing. I want you out of this shit! Do you understand? I want you out of it. What you did before you knew me is your business, but now it's different. I don't give a damn what you did before you knew me. You get out of this shit now, and you stay out! Do you hear what I'm saying, Zarah?'

I wasn't to know it then, but the next time someone shouted at me in this way would be in Evin Prison.

Behnam telephoned me the night following our argument, but I wouldn't speak to him. I felt ill with shock and disappointment. There was no question that I loved Behnam, but his outburst confused me. Love, in its nature, is hostile to change, even to alteration. In Shakespeare's famous sonnet, 'Love is not love/Which alters when it alteration finds', but I wonder how true that is. Love is deep, certainly; but so is conviction, including political conviction. I was ill, sick at heart, because the things that had the deepest hold on me were at war with my affections. When I made my speech about reform, I was not attempting to establish myself as fashionably radical. I was speaking about issues that seemed to me as crucial as love. Surely love is about the liberty of the soul, and my politics were also about the liberty of the soul. It would be true to say that I never thought my speech could lead to my being kidnapped in the heart of Tehran and hustled off to an interrogation cell; I did know that making such a speech meant trouble, but I thought it was trouble of the sort you can't avoid.

After that initial argument, we fought almost every day, Behnam and I. I defended myself; he attacked my politics. He wanted me to quit university and prepare myself for marriage. For me, that was out of the question. I was ready for romance, certainly, but I was by no means ready for the conventional sort of marriage that Behnam appeared to have in mind. Even asking me to quit university implied that he thought my education was utterly beside the point. Maybe he thought literature was a waste of time, too. What I wanted for our marriage, if we were to have a marriage, was kissing, hugging, and a great deal of reading. I imagined a solid wall of books before I imagined a nursery.

Our bickering was only ever suspended when Behnam answered his mobile. I would be sitting beside him, listening to him chat to well-known members of parliament, and sometimes to people so elevated in the regime that I was stunned at the ease of his conversation with them. I said to him once, 'Is that who I think it is?' Behnam responded by telling me that his business dealings had nothing whatsoever to do with me, or with us as a couple. All the while, I was developing a more complete comprehension of Behnam's true position within the business community. What I had at first been unwilling to concede – that Behnam was, for all intents and purposes, part of the regime – I grew closer and closer to admitting.

Behnam was quite willing to agree that Iran's unelected Council of Guardians, originally appointed by Khomeini, was the de facto ruler of the country, since they could reject any bill passed by the elected parliament. He would also concede that the regime was content to subvert the constitution in any way it liked; that it maintained a secret police force as disgraceful as Savak; that corruption within the higher echelons of the regime ran rampant; that women had less legislated freedom than slaves. None of this mattered to him; or, I should say, it didn't matter enough.

But no sooner had I admitted that the man I loved was in effect my political enemy than I began that process, common to women all over the world, I believe, which is supposed to conclude with the conversion of the beloved to one's point of view. Women marry alcoholics, telling themselves that they will change them, that love will change them; they marry wife-beaters, believing the same thing – the beloved fellow will see the light; they marry philanderers believing that constant affection and the daily evidence of one's devotion will see the beloved settle happily for blissful domesticity. It is almost an occupational hazard of being female, this profound conviction that love will bring about desired change. Perhaps it is a form of egocentricity. Perhaps there is a type of arrogance in women that compels them to believe that love is so vital that even a benighted fool will eventually give up his appalling habits. There is certainly no evidence to support this egocentric conviction anywhere in the world that exists here and now, nor in history. Setting one's better judgement aside to marry a man on the basis of one's convictions about the goodness in him rising to the top like cream on milk is surely a folly.

I took Behnam to political meetings. I gave him the chance to see the obduracy and intolerance of the regime. I introduced him to friends of mine who I thought might have the eloquence to persuade Behnam to a happier point of view. But he would leave halfway through the meetings, or get into bitter arguments with my friends. He was leading his own resistance movement against my personal reform movement. Finally, my friends begged me not to bring Behnam with me anymore. They were fed up with his captiousness and sarcasm and mulishness. At the same time, he helped the reform movement financially. This was generous of him, of course; but, in another way, it was not so generous. He was buying me off, in effect; he was saying, 'I'll do what I can with money but, really, I abhor your politics.'

My mother met him, and liked him well enough. And why wouldn't she? He was a man of tremendous influence. He could make a telephone call and get fines cancelled, disputes settled, parking tickets voided. He spoke on a daily basis to some of the most powerful figures in the nation about the importation of chemicals and about business in general, relaying information from his father in America, making arrangements to side-step trade embargoes. He wore a suit, he was well groomed, he spoke politely. My mother saw in him a protector for me; and when all is said and done, mothers everywhere are inclined to opt for sons-in-law who will provide for their daughters and keep them out of harm's way. And, of course, I had told her how much I loved him, so she was thinking of my heart, too.

My father hadn't met Behnam at this stage of our relationship;

I had the feeling that the meeting, when it came about, would be awkward, and I'd been avoiding it. Behnam, for his part, seemed to me to be happy to postpone any interview with Dad. The thing was, my mother was happy to see me marry into the establishment. But my father? He'd be far more critical of Behnam's links with the country's puppet-masters. It was politics, once again. For my father, political convictions were a crucially important feature of a man's (or a woman's) make-up. They were not something adopted for the sake of expedience; my father was no Iranian Vicar of Bray. And I was my father's daughter when it came to politics, although I placed the emphasis on personal liberty more pointedly than my father did.

The relationship stumbled along, dominated by bickering and disagreement. I had no intention of simply walking away from Behnam; but, at the same time, I found it impossible to imagine our life together. My mother, my brothers and sisters, my nephews, all took it as settled that I would marry Behnam and that we would make a terrific couple. After all, in Iran a young woman would not normally accept a suitor unless she intended to marry him; and although my family was less conventional in that way, it must have seemed to them that I would have to be insanely fussy if I didn't marry Behnam. For me, it was all a puzzle. I loved a man I could not marry, but I didn't have the character to simply stand up and declare with sincere pride that I could not commit myself to a marriage that would not make me happy.

In this desperately conflicted state, I was asked one day to accompany Behnam to a wedding party. The groom was one of his friends. I agreed to go, of course; one part of me wanted people to see us together as a couple. So I dressed in the way I would normally dress for such an occasion – modestly enough, but not conservatively. There were degrees of female religious observance in Iran, advertised by the severity of attire. One could dress to demonstrate the undiluted fundamentalism of one's husband, leaving barely a square centimetre of skin exposed, and one could dress to show proper respect for the statutes of the state without going overboard: a vestment worn to cover one's form from shoulders to lower-calf in any of a half-dozen fairly subdued colours; a scarf to cover the hair; a little lipstick; some eyeliner; some blush-on. Between these two extremes (so far as public exposure was concerned) lay a dozen variations. The choice of attire served roughly the same purpose as attire and grooming in many another society, including those in the West. What long hair and blue jeans were to kids in the United States in the 1960s, a pale-blue vestment, pale-green scarf, and pale-pink lipstick were to young women in 1990s' Iran.

So far, so good. I was dressed comfortably, and no one was likely to take offence. But on the way to the wedding party, Behnam stopped the car in an out-of-the-way place and produced an extremely orthodox version of a chador, such as only the most devout Iranian women wore.

'What's this?' I asked.

'I want you to wear this tonight,' said Behnam tersely, 'and I don't want a religious, political, historical, or any other kind of lecture about it. I want you for who you are, Zarah, but when we're with these people, we have to be like them. Okay? No ifs, no buts.'

I drew a sharp breath, looked at the uncompromising set of Behnam's jaw, thought about it for a half-minute or so, then capitulated. It was just for now, I promised myself.

At the party, all the women were dressed exactly like me. Anyone glancing at the small crowd of us conversing together and segregated from the men would have been hard-put to tell one woman from another. We were advertising, as a group, our satisfaction with the regime, with its rules and dogma, just as women at a Republican Party fundraiser in the United States would do now – particularly a fundraiser in the Bible Belt. No man would bother asking me (or any other woman at the party) my opinion on any political, social, or cultural subject. There would be no point; it would be assumed that I would endorse the government's and the clergy's position on everything: foreign policy, the obligations of Muslim women, the untold benefits to Iran of the Islamic Revolution. And it would be the same, I would imagine, at this fundraiser in the Bible Belt I have just plucked out of the air: any woman wearing an immodest Versace slip would be barred from entry; every woman could have her opinions on almost every issue assumed. But it vexed me almost to madness to know this. It made me ill. I wanted to scream, 'It's bullshit! I'm wearing this thing because I was made to!' I looked across at the influential men in the male salon, and I knew that some of them would have been responsible for imprisoning certain of my friends.

It was a farce, and I was a fraud. I took a deep breath, and walked straight into the male salon. All the men fell silent. I was stared at with as much astonishment as if I'd suddenly jumped onto a table and started dancing with my chador hitched up to my thighs. Behnam, distressed, apologised to the man he'd been talking to. 'Sorry, haji, she's my fiancée.' He took my arm and marched me out of the salon.

'What in God's name do you think you're doing? Do you know what reputation means?'

Behnam spoke in that tone of outraged conviction, so false, that I had learned to detest.

'I want to go home. I can't be here. I can't do this,' I said, struggling against my tears. He called me a cab and went back in to the party to mend his reputation. I cried all the way home. I thought, and believed, that we couldn't possibly be in love — as a matter of fact, that we hated each other. But the pain!

Behnam called me later that night. I told him I needed a break, time to think, and then hung up.

chapter nine

I have found a friend in the cell above me. His name is Ali Reza, and I know him from university. I heard his voice calling down through the ventilation grid that encloses the fan in the ceiling without knowing, at first, whose voice it was. It took me some time after he told me his name to make the connection. It's good to have someone I know nearby, but this consolation has its limitations: two powerless people can do little more than sympathise with each other, and of all forms of relief a person might crave in my situation, sympathy is the least availing.

What torments me more consistently than anything else is the thought of my mother left bereft of information about me. Ali Reza cannot help me get a message to my parents; I can't provide any real assistance to him. So all we can do is agree that we have come to a sorry pass, and one's appetite for complaint is soon exhausted. It is practical things that I find myself dwelling on in this cell: the need to get a message out is only the foremost longing; after that, such things as hygiene occupy my thoughts, the yearning to be clean. Something to read would be wonderful. I have the Koran, but it doesn't satisfy my hunger for news of the world. A chair to sit on would be a godsend. So would a comb, and pen and paper.

Today, Ali Reza wants to talk about my birthday party some months back. He was there at the party with his fiancée, Atefeh. Stretched out on the floor of my cell, I listen to Ali Reza's voice recalling the details of my party, filling my head with memories of dancing and laughter, music, and wonderful food like masst-o-khiar, minza ghasomi, khaviar, and kabab koobideh. The more Ali Reza recalls, the bleaker I feel. It is all so remote, that time of light and laughter. Is he trying to relieve my misery with his chatter? I should be grateful to him, but what I really want to tell him is to shut up, to please be silent about that time. If I were walking to a wall where a firing squad awaited me, maybe I would be content to acknowledge all the carefree periods of my life; maybe I would be ready, facing certain death, to make a reckoning, agree that I had known many of the best things in life. But here in this cell, I can't accept that my life is over; I can't settle down to a reckoning, give good fortune its due. Reminding me of happy times merely makes the concrete walls seem that much more impenetrable, the air in my cell that much more listless, and joy that much more distant. I begin to sob, and Ali Reza can hear me.

'What's wrong, Zarah? What's the matter?'

'No more!'

'What do you mean? Aren't we friends?'

'Yes, we're friends, but no more, please!'

Now my sobbing is out of control. Misery, I realise, is a weight, and its burden can be increased to the point at which one's legs buckle. Ali Reza, with all of his good intentions and his sweetness and concern for me, has been adding to the burden, and now my misery is complete. Oh God, I never had the strength for heroism, for politics. It's not in my make-up. I'm weak and cowardly. I should have left shouting in the streets to other people, stronger people. I hate politics. I hate protests. I hate it all.

———

Ali Reza has left me to myself. My tears have abated. I'm sitting on the floor, waiting for nothing at all to happen, or for another interrogation, or for nothing at all, or for another interrogation, or for nothing. I don't care. I can face it now. I'm hopeless, pathetic, a child sent on an adult's errand.

One of the female guards shouts through the hatch in my cell door, 'Shower time!'

At the sound of these words, every particle of my misery evaporates. It's like a gift. I almost feel as though I love the guard who has announced this blessing.

She drops the blindfold inside, and I leap to pick it up and slip it on. I feel ridiculously light-hearted. This will be my first shower in a week.

'You have ten minutes. Wash your underwear, too. Leave it on when you're showering.'

'Sure,' I say. 'Thank you. Thank you.'

When we reach what I take to be the showers, the guard pushes me forward. I can feel a wet surface under my feet. I remove the blindfold and find myself on a cement floor under a crude water outlet protruding from the concrete-brick wall. It's as pitiless a place as anywhere in Evin; but to me, so sick of the stink of my own body, it is heaven.

I shut the door before removing my prison tunic, then

abruptly jump as if a bare electrical wire had been jabbed into my back when the guard kicks the door open.

'Who told you to close the door?' she shouts. She is glaring at me as if her disgust is almost ungovernable; as if she might at any moment lose control and beat me with her fists. For what? How on earth was I to know the ludicrous rules of the shower block?

'Sorry,' I whimper.

I turn on the tap, and a thin trickle of warm water issues from the outlet. A well-used cake of green Golnar soap (the cheapest soap you can buy in Iran) is sitting on a ledge, and I immediately begin to scrub myself. My cuts and abrasions sting furiously, but I am desperate to clean them, to forestall infection. I soak my hair and attempt to wash it, but the meagre trickle of water and the coarseness of the soap make it difficult to create a lather. My hair is long and thick. At home (home!) my mother or my sister would help me dry it and brush it after a shower. Sometimes – the best times of all – my father would brush it for me, and tell me stories about his mother and how my hair was like hers. The luxury of his strong, even brushing! As I struggle with my hair in this rather slimy hole of a shower stall, I recall my father's voice singing Kurdish songs to me, wrapping me in a cocoon of enchantment and love. My favourite song of all was a Kurdish folk song about a pretty girl with long hair:

Dancing with shining hair, my pretty lover,
The sun is shining on her hair, my pretty lover,
It breaks my heart when she ties her hair up, my pretty lover ...

I whisper this song while I'm washing, but very, very quietly. Even though my face is wet, I can feel the special wetness of my tears brought on by the thought of never seeing my father again.

'Time is over!' the guard shouts.

She drops the blindfold on the floor beside me. As I bend to pick it up, I catch a glimpse of her face. She isn't old, but her weathered complexion and severe expression make her seem as if she is. She must be so practised in going the whole day without smiling. Perhaps she pities me, as I pity her. Perhaps she thinks me grotesque, ugly, a lost soul. As I tie on the blindfold, I find myself thinking about her, in a series of rapid thoughts, each lasting a fraction of a second: *Is she a mother? What are her kids like? Does she hate her job? Does she love her job? What is her name?* It is as if my mind is trying to satisfy a hunger for normal social interaction, normal curiosity. *Does she wonder why I am here? Does she think I have done something dreadful?* Or maybe she knows why I am here and considers protesting against the regime a frightful crime. Or maybe she simply doesn't care – has no opinion of me, no concern for me at all.

I have been given a clean prison tunic and clean prison underwear, after handing back my own wet underwear. It makes me happy to have showered, to be dressed in clean clothing, even if that clothing is just the drab, grey Evin uniform. My spirits soar. The guard grabs my arm more forcefully than she needs to, as if her contempt for me has been exacerbated by my having glimpsed her face. I don't mind. I don't fear her now. I have seen her face, and that makes so much difference.

Back in my cell, my cheerful mood survives. Any person in my situation, in whatever country that person suffers, under whatever regime, surely strives to create a haven, a secure corner. I'm sure that people in far more wretched circumstances than mine do just that. They look forward to the cold corner of a fetid cell, to a niche that a rat would think too filthy to pause in

— simply because, for a short time, the body, the mind, and the soul can converse, can offer each other comfort. My cell is two metres long by a metre-and-a-half wide. The door is iron. There are no windows. On the concrete ceiling a strip light burns constantly, maddeningly. There is no bed. It is a man-made cave, a very small one; but at times like this, I adore it. I can gather together the fragments that make up who I am, cram them back together, and become a person again.

My mood of foolish contentment is interrupted by the sound of the slot in my door opening. The blindfold is dropped through. I get up off the floor and slip it on. Strangely, I remain happy, even when the guard swings the door open and prods me forward along the corridor. I'm frightened as I always am when being taken for interrogation, but the fear is under control. Can it be that a shower has restored enough self-respect for me to have regained my courage? Is life that simple? Maybe it is that simple, because I find myself almost smiling as I stride along the corridor — yes, stride! — entertaining with perfect equanimity the possibility that I might be killed today. How might they kill me? Shoot me through the head? Let them.

'How are you today?' I ask the guard.

'Keep walking and don't talk!' he tells me shrilly.

His response withers my sense of conviction. How shallow it was! It had no roots. It was a fantasy. When will I stop doing this? When will I stop believing that the people who have charge of me here are nice people deep down, people who will respond courteously to a polite enquiry? I have to ask myself whether I'm mentally defective. It's my upbringing, of course — my religion. Be nice and people will be nice to me. Think nice thoughts. The thing is, it's not possible for me to accept evil at first glance. Perhaps not even at the second, the third, or the fourth glance.

For a person like me, evil has to insist and insist on itself, prove itself again and again. Otherwise, between episodes, I forget, woefully.

By the time I'm ordered to stop walking, I'm trembling again. All the resolve in my heart and stomach have vanished. The door is opened, and I'm pushed inside. As weak and pathetic as I felt just outside the door, I'm worse once in the interrogation room. A day-old chicken would have more strength and courage than I possess at this moment.

I hear the door closing. I hear footfalls approaching. It's the fat interrogator this time. I can smell him. It's not just his breath; it's his body, too. I shuffle forward in my blindfold. The interrogator gives me a prod, urging me in the direction of the chair, so it seems. I shuffle a few more steps and strike my knee on the chair. I feel my way into a sitting position.

'Did you have a shower?' he asks. 'You stank last time.'

He gives a little laugh, as satisfied as ever with his humour. It flashes through my brain to say something like, 'Oh, the pot is calling the kettle black!' (in Farsi, 'Two pots on the fire call each other black-face'), but I manage to keep my mouth shut.

The interrogator begins his slow, tormenting circuit of the room, coming closer to me, heading a little further away, returning again. I suppose the reason that he uses these tormenting tricks, which are so corny, is that they work.

'Are you going to tell me what Arash did to you when you went to his place?' he says, his mouth close to my ear.

'I told you before,' I answer, and turn my face away from his breath.

'Tell me again.'

'We're friends, university friends. That's all, I promise.'

He gives his little laugh again, slightly hoarse. Then he tells me that he has decided to help my memory work. He says he has prepared a list of all the things I have 'forgotten'. He tells me that he is going to leave the piece of paper before me on the desk, and that I am to put my signature on it. Before he goes, he says again that he expects my name on the paper by the time he returns.

When I hear him leave the room, I remove the blindfold, blink in the white light, glance at the closed door, lean forward and, without picking the paper up, read what is written on it. It is a confession, or a series of confessions. Using absurd clichés, it describes a sexual relationship between Arash and myself. It speaks of links between my friends at Tehran University and Communist Party cells operating in Iran. It describes the role played by 'foreign powers' in the student protest movement. It says that I am fully aware of the role played in the student movement by the 'communist anti-Iranian and anti-Islamic groups'. It names Arash as having 'embraced communism'. I feel quite divorced from what is written on the paper, as if it is all about someone else. It is only as I rapidly read through it a second time that I properly comprehend that it is *me* these stories refer to, *my* supposed actions and beliefs. Even then, the audacity of the stories overwhelms me. The sheer brazenness of the fabrications make me think of the fantastic lies that children sometimes tell their parents or teachers – lies so outrageous that the parent hoots with laughter.

Does the fat man honestly think that anyone would believe this nonsense for one minute? The confessions make me out to be a sort of Mata Hari – part spy, part whore. But then a slow anger begins to brew in my stomach; for as disgraceful as these lies are, this piece of paper is what the fat man and the police and the mullahs intend to wave under the noses of my friends and teachers, perhaps show to my parents, maybe even publish in a newspaper. An agonising shame is mixed in with my anger, as if somebody had submitted a sloppy, botched essay under my name to the teacher at university I most respect. I want to shout out a window to everybody in Tehran, 'It's not me! It's a trick! Please, don't anybody believe a word of it!'

And, in fact, I do scream, but not from a window. I scream crazily from my chair in the direction of the door. 'This is not the truth! It's not the truth! I'm not signing this, you bastard!'

There is no response for long seconds, then comes the knock on the door that is meant to remind me to replace my blindfold. But I don't replace it. The fat man walks into the room, glares at me, and slaps me hard across my face.

'You little fuck! Why aren't you wearing your blindfold?'

'Because I want to see your disgusting face!' I shriek.

He slaps me again, harder. Now he is moving rapidly in his fat way, rummaging in his desk for something. He lumbers back to me, grabs my arms from behind, and ties my wrists together with some sort of harsh twine.

'Asadi!' he yells, calling for the guard.

The guard flings the door open, looks at me, and then at the fat man. He stands holding the door open while the fat man leaves. I know absolutely that I have brought about something dreadful, that I am going to pay for my shouting and my anger. But I don't know in exactly what way. I am reduced to screaming for help, as if there is someone in the prison who will intercede for me.

The fat man is back. He is holding a pair of scissors, with the blades upright and agape.

I am mad with fear, and how I repent of my anger! I beg the fat man not to do whatever he has in mind. This is real begging, such as I have never uttered before in my life. He pays not the least attention to my pleas; but I repeat them rapidly, hysterically, because that is the only effort I can make on my own behalf, futile though it is. He pulls my scarf from my head, and takes handfuls of my long hair and chops at them with the scissors. He grunts as he cuts, and his breathing is harsher than ever – the breathing of a man harbouring heart disease. I reef my head about trying to duck the blades of the scissors, but my scope of movement is limited. I scream non-stop, like a little child in a fit of howling, completely uninhibited. My violent attempts to avoid the blades only result in injury; the tips of the blades nick my scalp painfully. The fat man's manner is rough and heedless, but he is not actually attempting to stab me with the scissor points; that's all my doing. Eventually, I stop resisting, stop thrashing about; I sit mute with humiliation.

When all the length has been taken from my hair, the fat man starts in with electric shears, pushing the blades roughly over my scalp. With my head bowed, I can see through the blur of my tears the locks of my hair strewn on the concrete floor. Ages pass, with the sound of the shears burring in my ears, and short hairs falling to the floor and gathering in a furry mass at the back of my neck. The shearing takes the humiliation I'm experiencing in this room to a deeper, more wrenching level. I'm like an animal in the hands of a man who could shear me or cut my throat with equal unconcern.

When the shearing is at last finished, the fat man steps back from me to study his work. I keep my head bowed. The courage to lift my eyes, to look this man in the face and show that I will remain in possession of my dignity no matter what he does – no, I do not have courage of that sort.

The guard puts the blindfold on my eyes, unties my hands,

and urges me to my feet. I have no strength to move my legs, and the guard has to part carry, part drag, and part push me back to my cell. I drop the blindfold out through the slot for him, then sink to the floor. My cheeks, my scalp, the flesh of my neck have all sustained cuts and nicks that sting madly. But the exhaustion and pain are not nearly as much of a concern to me as the absence of my hair. These people have changed the very look of me.

—

When the guard's steps recede, I moan Ali Reza's name and he answers. He knows that I've been to interrogation.

'Are you okay?'

Perhaps I had intended to tell him exactly what has happened to me; but when it comes to it, I don't want to tell him anything.

'Yes, yes, I'm okay.'

'What did they do to you?'

'Nothing. I'm fine, I'm okay.'

'Tell me please, what happened?'

'Nothing happened, nothing. Just another interrogation.'

'Did they hit you?'

'No. Everything's okay.'

Ali Reza gives up. It must be obvious to him that I am distressed, but he probably understands that it is not something I can give him an account of for the time being. It's not sympathy I crave at this time. I don't want to hear the voice of a man who can do nothing to alleviate my distress other than agreeing with me that the fat interrogator is a vile specimen of humanity. Where's the solace in that? What I need is my father, holding my head to his chest and stroking my head. But no, no — I would hate my father to see me like this. That would be the worst thing. I need someone who can provide me with something even more comforting — a key to the door of my cell, a second key to the door of the prison, a car to carry me to some place where the police and interrogators can never find me. But what I have to face is that miracles will not come about through wishing, or praying, or begging.

My whole body itches with the irritation of hairs that have fallen inside my prison tunic. My head feels ... wrong. Not on the inside — on the outside. I want my hair back. Nothing that has happened to me in prison has distressed me like the shearing of my head. And I know it is shallow. I know it is all to do with vanity. But I was pretty once. I liked being pretty. So what is this — a character-building opportunity? A chance to accept how superficial being pretty is? I don't want the opportunity! I want to be a pretty Persian girl dutifully attending to her studies and having nothing to do with politics. Nothing.

chapter ten

So much of what people believe about the world outside their own country seems to me the product of fatigue in some cases; of laziness, in others. In the Iran of my childhood and adolescence, people believed that America was a land of movie stars, warmongers, two-door refrigerators, big cars, and hardly anything else. I believed the same thing in childhood. I wasn't interested enough to acquaint myself with the detailed portrait, so I settled for the sketch. And what was England? The home of a kindly looking old lady who was said to rule the land as queen. And of the Beatles. In France, you would find the Eiffel Tower surrounded by people who ate frogs and snails. Australia was a nation of swimming champions and kangaroos. Only students and specialists have the time and the desire to study portraits, so people can't be blamed for their ignorance. Any life is dominated by local exigencies; and people, by their nature, are more concerned with their immediate neighbourhood than with regional and world neighbourhoods.

It would have been perfectly excusable in me if I had thought of my country, of which I had an intimate knowledge, as unique in the world – as indeed it is in certain respects. It would have been excusable if I'd believed that, in all the world, only Iran suffered under insanely dogmatic mullahs. But by the time I'd completed high school and a year at Tehran University, I had studied enough history to know that every country has its mullahs, every country has its dogmatists and zealots, every country has at some time brought down an iron fist on those who question, coax, condemn, criticise. I didn't know of the reign of Joseph McCarthy in early post-war America; I hadn't heard the term 'witchhunt' applied metaphorically. But I knew of other witchhunts, of other petty tyrants who detested wonder, imagination, enquiry, curiosity. In university, I studied Spanish as my major; I read the poetry of Garcia Lorca, I knew how he died, and in what circumstances. Lorca became the first hero of my adulthood.

My earliest hero was my father, and he remains a hero to me: my defender in family squabbles, of course, but, more importantly, the man who stayed in Iran to face whatever the Islamic Revolution might subject him to when he could easily have run away. But having a hero who is also your father rules out the complement of romance. Lorca was introduced to my Spanish class in the first year of university and, as soon as I read his poetry, I knew that he was the man for me. It was not that I wanted to fantasise over a wildly handsome Spaniard (who happened to be gay – not that I knew that), but rather that my developing sense of justice was nourished by the story (at least the short, less-complicated version) of his artistic and political commitment.

When I reflect on the psychological process that led me into the streets to shout and argue, I always get back to the word 'justice'. Like most children, I grew up with a very strong sense of justice. What outrages a child more than being accused of something she or he did not do? And what distresses a child more than being exposed to the possibility that bad people often win? My childhood stories, read to me by my parents, by my teachers, were stories of good people winning out in the end. It's the same the world over. Later, I learned that good people don't have it all their own way; later still, in early adolescence, that bad people very often *do* have it all their own way. But isn't it wonderful how the belief in justice endures?

For a number of my fellow Persians, justice was God. For me, at the age of nineteen, justice was the right of girls like myself to exercise their powers and abilities and talents without the interference of the clergy. My conception of salvation was therefore more human-scale than that of the mullahs. I wasn't interested in making cosmic claims; I wanted to be free to walk down the street with the wind in my hair. I wanted to go to the movies all by myself, if I felt like it. I wanted to make a choice of occupation from as extensive a list as the boys I knew. From the beginning, politics for me was personal, but not exclusively so. It never is, is it? The freedom to walk down the street with the wind in my hair wouldn't have meant a thing unless all Persian girls could do the same. It's not about creating privilege. How can liberty ever be a privilege?

Why was it Lorca amongst the Spaniards I learned about who so attracted me? Why not Dali or Buñuel? I suppose Dali's conception of freedom was simply too weird for me. I had no desire to dress up in a goat skin and smear my body with dung. Buñuel worked in images – arresting images, certainly – but I didn't have the intellectual sophistication to locate the argument in Buñuel. My idea of liberty was simpleñ enough to be thought primitive, almost. Political theories of history and class went over my head. But some numbskull of a boy in his late teens being licensed by the mullahs of my country to bully me when my scarf slipped back an inch too far off my forehead, to lecture me, menace me ... well, that was intolerable. And there were numbskulls of boys all over the place in Tehran when I was growing up: Basij, the citizens' militia of the regime, self-important little pains-in-the-neck poking their noses in everywhere, sniffing your breath for the tang of liquor, prying, pestering, firing off insults.

I have no doubt that, just as every country has its mullahs, every country has endured the reign of its own Basij. I think we have to accept the fact that the great majority of teenage boys are hopeless blockheads — and my apologies to the exceptions. Give them the right to persecute someone or some group, put a gun in their hands, a whip, a tarbrush, and away they go, full of righteous zeal and stupidity. The Basij was the Hitler Youth of Iran, and the Hitler Youth of Germany no doubt had its precursors in the Something Youth of Somewhere Else, and back and back to heaven knows when. Girls can be dim, too; I wouldn't wish to deny that — dim and brutal. But in Iran, one's experience is mostly of the dimness of boys.

Lorca wasn't an egomaniac. Lorca wasn't an ideologue. He was a poet, and that was his great attraction:

I have shut my windows
I do not want to hear the weeping
But from behind the grey walls
Nothing is heard but the weeping
There are few angels that sing
There are few dogs that bark
A thousand violins fit in the palm of the hand
But the weeping is an immense angel

The weeping is an immense dog
The weeping is an immense violin
Tears strangle the wind
Nothing is heard but the weeping

What impressed me in this poem was the sensibility of a man, a poet, who could actually hear the weeping. Because the weeping goes on everywhere, and not everyone can hear it. The weeping can fill a room, and be unheard by the people sitting and talking. To hear the weeping, your ears must have perfect pitch for the sounds of sorrow.

In my freshman year at Tehran University, my class performed a version of Lorca's play *Llerma*. We made a good job of it. The Spanish ambassador came to the university theatre to see the production, and congratulated us. I read as many of Lorca's plays and poems as I could lay my hands on; and while I read, I sensed the quickening of that sense of justice I spoke about. Not that the stories were political diagrams; far from it. But I absorbed the sensibility of the mind behind the stories and poems: a sensibility that created vivid images of struggle, of the soul's imprisonment, and of freedom. The struggle was for liberty; that was how I conceived it.

I think most people who one day find themselves shaking their fists at the mullahs of their country first find a person (often a writer) who helps them define what they mean by liberty. For many, that person will be a political theorist – such as Marx – but not always. It is quite possible to locate a guide in a poet such as Omar Khayyam of Naishapur, or in Sa'adi, or Hafiz – poets who wrote of sadness, loss, the casual cruelty of the cosmos, love, desire. Even when the subject is disguised, I always feel that the real theme of good poetry is liberty. I have never read a fine poem or story that celebrated repression, and that rejoiced in the unfettered power of mullahs.

—

The liberty of language had found its way into my heart years before Lorca came into my life. I had enjoyed reading from childhood; but in my teens that enjoyment underwent the first of two transformations and became a type of addiction. It might have been hormonal. Fevers get into the blood of girls in puberty. In another country, I might have become one of those kids at pop concerts, trembling and shrieking and shedding tears and reaching out to young men strutting on stage. I read in a state of ecstatic transport — novels, film magazines, newspapers, books on politics. I made little distinction so far as quality and merit went; I could get as excited by an essay in my high-school philosophy textbook as by the copy in magazine advertisements. Every surface in my bedroom was smothered in words on paper.

My mother didn't like it at all. She had nothing against reading, but she could tell from the distracted look of me that my addiction was liable to twist me out of shape, turn me into a freak. She would remind me that I would one day be a grown woman and a wife, and asked what my household would look like if all I ever did was read. To calm her down, I forced myself to give a certain amount of time to the time-honoured crafts of the Persian wife: I sewed and embroidered, and helped out with the cooking and the preparation of meals. I gave every appearance of a girl thinking ahead to home life and home duties, but it was all a fraud.

I was like a heroin addict who learns how to appear supremely in control and perfectly able to negotiate a day-to-day existence while scheming for the opportunity to introduce madness into her veins. I made sure that books my mother would approve of – library books on running a household, pleasing a husband, cleaning rugs and carpets, preparing a picnic lunch for a day in the park, recognising the signs of ailments in infants – were always on top of my piles of books, or that these wholesome volumes were the ones that had their spines facing outwards on my shelves. More concealed were the books by Sadeq Hedayat and Jamalzadeh, great heroes of contemporary Persian literature, both novelists and both truly subversive of authority in their politics and their insistence on employing simple, clear prose. My mother knew of the Hedayat and Jamalzadeh books, but she believed that they were of less importance to me than the books which she approved of. Or maybe it was just that she was touched by my willingness to make it appear that way. After all, a person who takes pains to spare your fears and concerns must love you, mustn't she? Not that my mother was in any doubt about my love for her.

Hedayat and Jamalzadeh did not frighten my mother nearly as much as Kafka and Sartre did. When the works of these authors appeared in my room, late in my high-school years, my mother made it clear that she believed I was in serious danger of turning into an unmarriageable intellectual. She despaired of me, threw up her hands, and asked aloud if there were some special reason that, of all the mothers in Iran, she had been given a daughter who couldn't tell a crochet-hook from a cooking pot. But I hadn't abandoned the aspirations of other girls my age; I still longed for the love of a good man, for marriage and family. At the same time, the poets, novelists, and philosophers I was reading so avidly had created a more complex world for me to inhabit. I was reading to educate myself about the way the world worked. I wanted to know that. I wanted to uncover the irreducible truth.

At sixteen, my experience of reading underwent its second transformation. I was no longer able to think of reading as 'fun'. The enjoyment it gave me was a new sort of enjoyment; it was not the beauty of the words that thrilled me now (although that could still happen), but their meaning. The way I had enjoyed literature up until the age of sixteen was related to love – strong feelings, yes, even feverishly strong feelings, but tempered by joy, tenderness. My new way of enjoying books was more like passion – dangerous, consuming and, although you would die for it, unlikely to lead to happiness. It was like waking up one morning and finding that the sky was no longer blue, but red. Instead of fretting about the loss of blue skies, you simply say, 'Yes, the sky should be red and, from now on, only red skies will do for me.' Somewhere within, though, the reader you once were begins to mourn for you, attempts to warn you that you should not turn your back on blue skies and happiness so readily.

My mother began to look at me as if I were perhaps in need of medical attention.

What was happening to me was something that happens to teenagers everywhere, or to some of them: the lessons of my reading, the lessons of my observations of the people around me and the world around me, the insistent voices in my head and heart and soul, were all striving to unite around a theme to carry me into adulthood. I know that the theme which many teenagers in some Western countries now arrive at is not that complex: *make a good living, and enjoy yourself the livelong day*. But in those same countries at other times – in the 1960s, for example – the theme was less self-interested. For me, the theme I was searching for was given focus by Lorca, then by the Basij. But it was only when I saw my cousin in hospital in Shiraz, with most of her skin burnt from her body, that I truly developed a conviction about justice.

The girl, my cousin, was living in a village in the west of Iran. She had been very young when she married a man from Tehran, only fifteen, full of enthusiasm at the prospect of living in a big city. Now, only a few months into her marriage, she had doused herself in petrol and put a match to her clothing. I went to her room to visit her at the Burns and Trauma Hospital in Tehran. The smell of cooked meat was so strong that I had to fight the urge to throw up. According to the doctors, she had received burns to 85 per cent of her body. The unburnt 15 per cent included her lips circling her startlingly white teeth. I recalled her wonderful smile on those occasions in the past when we had visited her and her family on their farm. She'd been such a happy kid, full of laughter, always showing those brilliant teeth. I'd thought of her as one of those people for whom joy was a normal state of being.

There was very little that I could say to my cousin. The usual, comforting clichés one would offer to a patient were obviously out of the question: 'Get well soon'; 'Don't worry, you're in good hands'. All the while, I was thinking about her motive. If you saturate yourself in petrol and strike a flame, you are not simply crying out for help; you are crying out for death.

Sometime later I saw a semi-documentary film by Daryoush Mehjuie set in Ilam, a city in the west of Iran where ten girls and young women commit suicide each month. Ilam is not exceptional; suicides amongst young women are frequent in all regions of Iran. But the method chosen by young women in Ilam and in the region that surrounds Ilam — self-immolation — is exceptional; elsewhere in Iran, young women poison themselves, drown themselves, hang themselves, leap to their deaths. The suggestion of Daryoush Mehjuie's film is that a type of macabre tradition has grown up amongst distressed young women in the region that somehow or other commends self-immolation as the preferred means of ending one's life – as if each successive suicide honours the choice of death-by-fire of all the others who have gone before. In this way, a type of sisterhood is established. Self-immolation becomes a serial suicide note – each victim saying, in effect, 'My motive is the same as she who went before.' There is no question of murder in these cases (unlike in India, where countless young women are put to death in this way by relatives). In Ilam and the Sunni western region, these young women have chosen death-by-fire over life. I don't know where the tradition came from, and why it is so local. It may be atavistic, harking back to an ancient and violent worship of fire in pagan times – the worship to which Zoroastrianism gave a more beneficent expression.

Why do these young women kill themselves? So far as the film-makers could see, and so far as I could see, the motive is the intolerable disappointment generated by growing up with a head full of dreams and desires that have so little chance of being fulfilled. My cousin and I would lie down in the grass on her father's farm, and she would ask me how boys and girls in Tehran get to know each other and become friends. She asked me if I had kissed a boy yet. She asked if I agreed that Mehdi Mahdavi Kia, an Iranian international football player, was handsome. She said she would love to see him close-up one day. She spoke about love and romance and kisses and the gallantry she might one day encounter in a suitor as handsome as Mehdi Mahdavi Kia. Her imagination bubbled with spiritual ambition and erotic longing.

Although I would now be inclined to say that my cousin's ambitions were hopelessly unrealistic, do I really have the right to say that? What was she hoping for, after all? A palace of gold, eternal bliss, the devotion of a prince? No. What she hoped for was the love of a good man, and the chance to express her own love. That's not asking for the moon and stars. Except that, for many young women in Iran, and in many other countries – many! – it *is* asking for the moon and stars. The man you marry, who may have been chosen for you by your parents, may be a stranger to you at the marriage ceremony; a stranger a month later; a stranger ten years later; a stranger forever. Not always, of course. You may win the lottery. Many Iranian men have fine qualities to offer a woman; I've personally met a number of them, especially at university, sometimes in the bazaar. But there are only so many winners of lotteries, and the odds against winning are longer, surely, when girls and young women from poor families (in particular) are matched with much older men, or with men who have not been prepared by their upbringing and culture to pay much attention to what the child they have wedded would wish to have coaxed from her heart.

There is a saying that has its origin in the poetry of Byron, 'Love to a woman is life itself; to a man, it's a thing apart.' The Persian equivalent would be, 'Woman's love is the flight of a bird; man's, the roar of a lion'. Whatever the yearnings and hopes of these young women at one stage of their lives, I fear that, at the moment the flame touches their garments, love to them is what Cordoba is to the traveller in Lorca's poem, 'Song of the Horseman':

Cordoba,
Distant and alone.

ZARAH GHAHRAMANI

Black pony, big moon,
Olives in my saddlebag.
Though I know these roads,
I'll never reach Cordoba.
Through the plains, through wind,
Black pony, red moon, death watching me
From the high towers of Cordoba.
Ay! What a long road.
Ay! What a brave pony.
Ay! Death, you will take me,
On the road to Cordoba.

The sight of my cousin's body, dressed in white bandages except for her lips and eyes, made me so furious that, when I saw her father weeping at the hospital, I didn't know if my pity could subdue my anger. 'Do you know what has happened to your friend?' he asked me, torn apart by pain.

Did I know what had happened to my friend? Yes! She was married when she was a child. She was a wife when she was a child. She was an object of lust when she was a child. She had her daydreams dismissed forever when she was a child. She had the spring of life within poisoned at its source when she was a child. She had her soul thieved from her when she was a child. But could I say this to her husband? No. If he were capable of understanding what I might have said, he would not have married this child to begin with. So I wept with him, regardless of my anger, then returned to my cousin's room. Again, the smell of her cooked body overwhelmed me.

That day of the visit to my cousin, I was scheduled to play basketball with my team. Basketball was my great physical consolation for the maddening things my mind was doing to me.

How I loved to play! The camaraderie with my team-mates, the affection I felt for our coach and, yes, the lust for victory in a field of endeavour where victory – simple, satisfying – was at least a possibility! So I went to play basketball after going to the hospital, hoping that the vigour of the game would get the image of my cousin out of my brain for a time. But it wasn't like that. I walked onto the court in a state of rage. I didn't talk to anyone, except to shriek at them whenever I missed a pass or they missed a pass to me. Sima, our coach, took me out of the game and wouldn't let me back on the court until the game was over.

I waited until everyone was gone, or so I thought. Then I took the ball and ran up and down the court, up and down, over and over, firing the ball into the wall and shouting and howling. When, at last, I was too exhausted to continue, I stopped and changed into my street clothes. It was then that I noticed Sima sitting by herself in the stand. She'd been watching me patiently. I didn't say a thing to her – just grabbed my bag and left the stadium and walked out into the streets of Tehran.

It took ten days for my cousin to die. I cried and howled for the whole of those ten days; but when it was announced that she was dead I sighed with relief, and my eyes stayed dry.

chapter eleven

The interrogator nudges me toward the chair. I can feel the edge of the seat against the backs of my legs. He pushes down on my shoulders, and I sink to a sitting position. This is the first interrogation since my hair was shorn. I am especially anxious, not knowing what further humiliation might follow. Is there a list of punishments, perhaps? Has it all been worked out scientifically? The list might commence with verbal abuse, then graduate to physical abuse, sexual abuse, shearing – then what? More ancient methods of torture? Does the interrogator have implements at his disposal? If so, I will tell him anything he asks me. I have already made this agreement with myself. I have conceded that I haven't the bravery or the conviction to endure anything of that sort. I have forgiven myself in advance.

The interrogator has nothing to say for a time. He lets me sit in silence. He isn't circling me, as he has on other occasions. So far as I can tell, he is simply watching me from his chair on the other side of the desk. Just being stared at in this way is obviously calculated to create tension. Every nerve in my body is exhorting me to prepare myself for something – a slap or a punch – but it is not possible to make this preparation when I can see nothing. I am beginning to understand the thinking behind everything the interrogator does. This in itself is a form of paranoia. I can't believe in the innocence of any action. For all I know, the interrogator might be sitting in front of me thinking of what he had for dinner, or picking his nose, or even wishing he was somewhere else – maybe watching a soap opera on television, or even reading stories to his children, if he has any. But I can't help attributing a motive to every single innovation of his approach. Perhaps I even credit him with more brains than he has.

'What an insistent mum you've got!' the interrogator says, out of the blue. The first thing I register is that this is not the fat man but the other one; the one whose face I haven't seen. Then I comprehend that he is talking about my mother. It sickens me instantly that he should feel himself entitled to refer to *my* mother in the familiar manner as 'mum'. It is as if someone preparing to rape me should have the temerity to refer to what he is doing as 'making love'.

'My mother?'

'Yes, your mum comes here every day. She begs the guys at the gate for news of you. We tell her we've never seen you, never heard of you.'

I think of words I can't utter – 'vile, disgusting creature' – but it is not out of fear of punishment that I keep my mouth shut; it is because this is what he is looking for. I am trying to control my anger. I can see with perfect clarity in my mind's eye what my mother would look like pleading at the gate of Evin for news of me: her eyes wet, her lips all pale in that way they go when she is full of anxiety, her beautiful face distorted. And here it is all over again – my wretched naivety, my stupidity. I sit here expecting something bad, but it never occurs to me that they will use my mother's misery as a weapon of torture. Can I ever, ever, *ever* learn that these people will use anything in the world to cause me pain, that they don't draw a line anywhere? What has to happen to me before I can get it through my head? Do they have to cut my throat before I come to comprehend their malevolence?

'Because she knows that I'm here?' I ask softly.

The interrogator gives a single-syllable laugh. 'But you aren't here, are you? No one is here.' Then he laughs more freely, probably because of the appalled expression on my face. My hatred for him at this moment is so intense that images of his face flash through my mind – a face that I have never seen. I see the face of a baboon, then of a jackal. I see lips flecked with spittle. I see rotted stumps of teeth like rocks in the desert. I see eyes devoid of shame, like those of some ancient whore plying her trade in the grimy streets of Gonrok in West Tehran. This is what I'm reduced to: melodrama, as if I were a princess in the cave of an ogre.

'I need some information from you,' the interrogator says with no special emphasis, as if we were in an office and there was just a small matter to be cleared up. He puts a series of questions to me, all to do with the recent student protests at Tehran University that I took part in; protests that focused on the dismissal and imprisonment of two professors, one of them a favourite of mine who taught a version of Iran's history that was unacceptable to the regime. The interrogator wants to know how I find out about the meetings at which the protests are organised. Who informs me and the other students when a meeting is to take place? Do we have secret passwords? Then he begins to ask questions about discussions at the meetings.

His questions are now highly detailed. He appears to know exactly what is spoken of at the meetings. He knows who opens them, and who makes suggestions at them. He knows what those suggestions are. His information is so accurate and comprehensive that, in fact, he has no need to ask me any questions about the meetings. His purpose is to let me know that what I thought was a secret kept by no more than four of five people is not a secret at all. He wants me to ask myself who the spy in our group is. And that is exactly what I do – question who the spy might be. Or is it possible that other members of our group have been picked up and interrogated, and that all of the details he is using now come from one of our number? Even as he nags at me with his questions, I study mental images of faces. Was it her? Was it him? Not one of them would say a thing, I'm certain. Not one of them would break down, even under torture. But is this true? I am myself ready to capitulate if the pain becomes too great. Why should I believe that the others are so much stronger than me?

'Did he ask you to cancel the classes?' the interrogator asks.

'Who?'

'That son of a bitch who was kicked out of university. Did he make you do it?'

'My professor?' I ask.

'Yes, the bastard who brainwashed you all, the one who was teaching you crap. That one.'

'You're the one talking crap, not him,' I snap. The words are out of my mouth before I can stop them. Within a split second, I repent. I will recant instantly if he demands it.

I hear his chair scrape on the floor. He is on me, grabbing my neck from behind. He shakes me, then pushes me forward. I topple from the chair and, as I fall, hit my chin on the edge of the table in an awkward way so that the flesh splits open. Even as I hit the floor I can feel blood flowing.

'Bitch!' he says. 'You talk shit, nothing but shit. You better learn to shut up, fool.'

It's a struggle, but I manage to get to my knees. I feel for the chair and put it upright on its legs, then sit on it, facing what I hope is forward. I touch my chin, feel the split flesh. The blood oozes over my fingers. 'Shit, shit, shit,' I hiss.

'Is that what you learned from him? Being a hardcase bitch? Yes? Before I get angry, answer my question. Did he ask you to cancel the classes?' he says.

'No, he didn't!'

'How did you inform everyone? How did everyone know that there would be no classes that day?'

'I don't know,' I answer wretchedly. 'I suggested it at the meeting and everyone agreed. That's all.'

'How would all the students know about it? The ones who weren't at the meeting? How would they know?'

'They just tell each other. We never make any announcement, never write anything down. They just told each other, that's all.'

'Is that right?' he says. I am about to say, 'Yes,' when he slaps me across the face. The split in my chin widens and the blood streams down my throat. I'm whimpering now like a child.

'Please take me to my cell!'

He doesn't answer. Instead, he begins a relentless series of questions – some of which he has asked before, some of which are new. Who was in charge? Who organised the cancellation of classes? How frequently did I meet with my friends? The questions come at me so rapidly that I can't keep up. Sometimes when I think I am answering one question, I realise that the interrogator has moved on to the next one. I am falling into a trance, unable to keep straight in my head what it was I really did in the protest movement and what I am being accused of. What is true and what is a lie are merging in my mind; but, worse than that, it all seems hopelessly unimportant. Where is my conviction? Have I ceased to believe in anything? I haven't even got a firm sense of myself as a human being. All that my body is capable of is recording pain, and my mind is like some crude, primitive device that can register nothing other than exhaustion. I answer, 'Yes' to whatever I'm asked. Did I cancel the classes? Yes, I cancelled the classes. Was I instructed to cancel the classes? Yes, I was instructed to cancel the classes. Yes to anything you ask. Yes, yes, yes.

Then, into the fog of pain and self-disgust, comes a much more vivid fear: that the split on my chin will become infected in this feculent place. I will not be given any medical treatment, I will not be given antiseptic, the wound on my chin will suppurate, I will become deformed and ugly, I will no longer be a pretty Persian girl, people will pity me, boys will avoid me, I will never marry. How powerful my vanity is! My world is toppling in ruins around me, and the only thing I can think of is my pretty face!

'Can I please go to the toilet?' I ask, but the interrogator persists with his questions. I am becoming drowsy, as if the interrogator were a hypnotist – not one who relies on the repetition of a visual image, but on the repetition of a sound.

I continue to answer like a talking metronome, wondering why the interrogator can be bothered believing me. Can't he see that my brain is shutting down? In my drowsiness, I think of the time I cut my right arm badly as a child and had to have the wound stitched. The doctor said, incorrectly, that I would not be able to use my right hand anymore; that I would have to write with my left hand. My father was away on a trip, and both my mother and I knew how upset he would be when he came home and saw me marred in this way. I was his pet, his favourite, his princess. And, sure enough, when he came home he was maddened by the idea of me being hurt and distressed; he took me against his chest and patted me for ages, murmuring words of love and comfort. Here I sit, sick with fatigue, sustaining myself in the very limited way I can by recalling the tenderness of my father, while at the same time relinquishing any pretence I had of honest conviction. What I really want of my father is for him to walk through the door, and to pick me up and say in his most commanding manner, 'You will leave this child alone from this point on. I will not permit you to harm her again. I will not permit you to ask her one question more. She is my child. I am her father.'

A further age passes before the interrogator calls the guard. I am being taken back to my cell. I ask the guard to let me use the toilet on the way. I wash my chin at the sink, lifting my blindfold to do so. But I make sure not to look at my reflection in the mirror. My ugliness would destroy what little self-esteem I have left.

—

Back in my cell, I sit thinking of Ali Reza in the cell above. And what I am thinking is this: *Ali Reza is the spy. That was why he was put in the cell above me. That is why he is forever questioning me. It is Ali Reza.* I address him in my mind with the harshest words I can summon. I excoriate him. I call him a coward, a jackal. But then it dawns on me that this is exactly what the interrogator wants me to think. He wants me to doubt everyone. What a playground my mind is for these people, these torturers! They pull my thoughts apart, then put them back together in a way that amuses them.

Maybe Ali Reza is thinking the same thing about me – that I am a spy. Maybe all the people in our group are doubting all the others.

At this moment, I am glad that Ali Reza is not calling to me from his cell. He must be away at interrogation; or, if he is the spy, he must be away reporting to his masters, receiving instructions. I detest myself for my distrust but, now that it has been switched on by the interrogator, I can't switch it off.

I must sleep. It's important.

As soon as I close my eyes, I hear a groan from Ali Reza's cell above. I attempt to ignore it, but it is repeated. Finally I stand up and place myself as close to the fan grille as possible.

'Ali Reza, is that you?'

No response.

'Is that you, Ali Reza? Hello? Ali Reza?'

'Who the hell is Ali Reza?' a voice answers. It is not Ali Reza's voice. I stand in silence, perplexed. A few minutes ago, I didn't want to hear from Ali Reza; now I feel bereft that he is not where he should be.

'I'm in the lower cell,' I whisper. 'Who are you? Why are you moaning?'

'Because I want to. What's it to you?'

Such a rude person! Who on earth is he?

'I've just had a long interrogation,' I tell this ill-mannered man. 'I'd be able to sleep if you'd keep it quiet.'

'So sleep, it's none of my business,' he says.

'I can't if you keep moaning!'

'I'll moan as much as I want,' he says. 'Prison isn't for you, father, is it?'

'Father'? What on earth is the matter with this moron?

'Fucking bitch, I don't know what she wants from me,' he

mutters, and goes on muttering. I listen in amazement. This guy is a genuine lunatic, and yet he's oddly fascinating to me. I hear him shuffling about and abusing me ceaselessly, as if in the space of a few seconds I have become a great burden to his existence. And what in God's name has become of Ali Reza? Does his disappearance confirm my doubts about him? Or should it quash them?

'Hey, you,' I whisper. 'Whoever you are, I'm as unlucky as you, believe me. Why can't you just be nice? I promise I won't even say hello to you anymore, but you should stop moaning, okay?'

'What have you done to be interrogated? Are you one of the protestors? A communist, are you?'

He doesn't appear to understand the rules of clandestine communication. He talks as loudly as if he were hailing me from across the street.

'I don't know who I am anymore – maybe someone like you.'

'Are you in here because of a cheque, too?' he asks.

'What on earth are you talking about? Cheque? Do you mean cheques like bank cheques?'

'None of your business,' he says.

'God, just go to sleep, okay? And you're right. It's none of my business.'

He starts moaning again. It sounds as if he's calling someone's name, but I can't understand him properly. I'm too tired to listen any longer. I climb under my blanket on the floor and close my eyes.

'Leila! I'll kill you when I'm free!' he yells.

I shut my ears to his craziness, and fall asleep.

When I wake, I hear the madman kicking on the door of his cell and screaming obscenities at the country's political leaders –

at Khamenei, Rafsanjani, Khatami. It's as if they are his personal enemies rather than his political foes. An outburst like this can have only one ending; and, sure enough, within a minute I hear the guards thudding down the corridor above and crashing open the cell door. I doubt if so much as a second has passed between the opening of the cell door and the beginning of the beating. I hear the thud of blows landing one after another, the shrieks of the madman, and the grunts of the guards. I can't tell what they are beating him with — maybe truncheons or maybe their fists. I curl myself into a ball under my blanket and jam the palms of my hands tightly over my ears. It makes no difference. The beating goes on and on and on. If it weren't for the sound of the madman's shrieks and gasps, I would think him dead. Dear God, didn't he know that this would happen?

I think a half-hour has passed without any break in the sound of the beating. Can anyone live through this? I'm shaking all over, like a child compelled to watch a horror movie.

At last, the cell door above slams shut. For some minutes, there is barely a sound to be heard. He is surely dead; at the very least, unconscious. Tentatively, I whisper, 'Are you alive?'

The madman begins moaning, in exactly the way he was moaning earlier. He doesn't reply when I repeat my question.

'Hey, sir, are you all right?' I ask again.

I can feel a type of hysteria building, as if the madman's moaning has infected me.

'I will cry if you don't stop!' I shriek.

The madman stops. But as soon as he falls silent, howling breaks from my mouth. I can't stop. I'm convulsed with fear, mixed with longing for my father's touch. I let the howling have its way.

chapter twelve

I was in the fourth grade at Reza Zadeh Primary School in south-central Tehran when a decree banning the wearing of white socks to school was announced. Iran was just emerging from its savage war with Iraq at the time; and, as is the case with almost all nations in time of war, those in power define and redefine what is to be accepted as patriotic behaviour. In essence, the rules amounted to this: the more unreflecting one's acceptance of the latest tests of patriotism, the better for that person. There was nothing new about this; it was just the same in Sparta during the Peloponnesian Wars. And there is, in fact, an insidious logic underlying tests of patriotism: those who don't or won't comply in effect identify themselves as subversives, and can be dealt with more easily. In Chile during the rule of the junta, teenagers who wore sneakers identified themselves as sympathisers with the left, and thereby became targets of the death squads who cruised the streets of Santiago. The sneaker rule was not even a decree; nevertheless, people were expected to know that the wearing of sneakers was offensive to the regime.

In Iran under the rule of the mullahs, everything was (and remains) politicised – even the colours of the rainbow. (This was the argument of the great Iranian film *Gabeh* (*Rug*) made by Majlis Majlisi in 1994.) There is no saying who in the regime came up with the idea of banning the wearing of white socks by schoolchildren. But one day it was announced by our principal that children who wore white socks to school were mocking the blood of the martyrs who had given up their lives fighting the Iraqis. It was not as though white was considered a particularly cheerful colour in Iranian culture; it has, by and large, the same association in my culture as in many others: purity, cleanliness, virginity. So I imagine that the pious law-makers simply thought that black was the only colour which adequately honoured the war martyrs. White became, in their minds (I'm only guessing, of course), the new pink.

When the announcement was made at the school assembly, every kid who had worn white socks that day – and even those who weren't sure – glanced down at their feet. Gasps and cries filled the air. We in white socks were horrified at what we had done. We'd blasphemed! We'd insulted young men who'd bled on the battlefields! But we knew that we hadn't intended to do any such thing. Kids pleaded to the teachers watching over us, 'Miss, I didn't know! Oh please, Miss, it wasn't my fault!'

You could sense the hysteria. Not one single child at my school had ever deliberately insulted 'the martyrs'; it would never have occurred to us to do so. And yet here we were, trembling with fear, our hearts pounding, because somehow or other, by some scheme of the Devil's, we had been made to *appear* unpatriotic, unrighteous, and un-Iranian. The principal had to intervene quickly and assure us that the decree only applied from the date of its announcement, which was a great relief because it was by no means out of the question in Iran for tests of patriotism to be back-dated.

So we went home that day and told our parents about the white-socks decree. The responses of parents would have been different in different households. In my household, there was a certain amount of eye-rolling. My father was, of course, disgusted. He was — and remains — a good Muslim, but he objects to his religion having irrational convictions foisted on it, such as the white-sock business. To him, Islam is the great solace of a people, not a bruising avalanche of mindless decrees. My mother simply absorbed the news, and made sure that I had good, patriotic socks of solid black to wear to school each morning.

You would think that the fear that had run like wildfire through the school assembly on the day of the announcement would have guaranteed that no child would ever again come to school in white socks. But, in the way of these things, there were lapses. Perhaps some parents forgot, or maybe after a few weeks the kids began to wonder whether such a decree had ever really been announced; maybe they had only dreamed it. Well, the school took the decree seriously, and the offenders were punished severely. The sentence could take the form of corporal punishment (administering the cane, just as in English public schools when wretched boys made a mistake of comparable inanity), but the most feared sanction was public shaming. The transgressors were told that they would have to 'answer our martyrs in the after-life' — a terrifying thing to have on your conscience.

In the immediate aftermath of the decree, I began to question just a tiny bit whether the martyrs were really going to be offended by white socks. After all, they were in heaven. Were they going to leave off whatever wonderful activities they were enjoying in heaven to weep over a negligent schoolchild? But my doubts were easily subdued. What I wanted to do as much or more than any other kid in my school was demonstrate my ability to follow rules with scrupulous attention. I was a goody-goody, probably the chief of all goody-goodies at Reza Zadeh, and I wanted it to be known that any other kid, even on his or her best day, could not get close to me in the exhibition of commendable behaviour.

During the ten days of the Dawn Celebration, commemorating the period between the return to Iran of Ruhallah Khomeini in 1979 and the birth of the Islamic Republic, each class had to prepare a program honouring the Father of the Nation and his great achievement. We sang revolutionary songs, acted out dramas of praise, and wrote stories that identified the sins of the Pahlavi era. Although we didn't know it, we were part of a worldwide congregation of children, all offering up our songs of praise to honour self-proclaimed messiahs, or the Stars and Stripes, or this or that magnificent battle, this or that glorious revolution. And all of us children in this congregation had villains to boo, a Goldstein to burn in effigy.

The offerings of each class were presented in the morning, before regular classes began, always out in the school quadrangle. The Ayatollah had returned to Iran in the month of February, and so the programs had to be performed in the cold and wet of that winter month. We didn't complain openly, but in every heart there dwelt a secret wish that the Father of the Nation had waited a few months longer before returning to his homeland.

The triumph of the Islamic Revolution didn't mean a great deal to me, nor to any of the kids I knew. (There were a few honourable exceptions.) But the Dawn Celebration did provide a wonderful opportunity for me to show how clever I was, and how obedient. I wrote articles that took a cudgel to the Pahlavis, even though my dad certainly would not have approved, since he remained a little sentimental about the Shah. I never showed him my writings, for this reason.

By the time I reached high school I was still very active in displaying my cleverness and in accepting pats on the back; but, all the while, the seed of doubt that the white-socks decree had planted in my mind was putting down fine roots. A sense of justice can always benefit from a complementary sense of the ridiculous. This was merely puzzling to me at the age of ten; but by the age of fourteen it was ludicrous. My friends and I found relief from the burden of listening in solemn silence to utter nonsense by whispering what we thought of as extremely witty jokes to each other. Isn't it both strange and wonderful that people in countries all over the world who are required to sniff platefuls of manure and pronounce them a delight to the nostrils retain the desire to speak the truth? This seems to have been especially true behind the Iron Curtain in the years of the Russian hegemony, and it was certainly true in Iran. We kids ridiculed the super-pious amongst us – not really the pious pure and simple, but the politically pious. The joy of being able to laugh at the laughable, to ridicule the ridiculous! It guards one's integrity when all other defences are proscribed. Of course, one should not go through one's life merely making fun of political pieties; that would be bad for the soul. But, at certain times, it saves us from the corruption of prescribed belief.

Fear enfeebles conviction, obviously; the cost of saying what you believe is often too high a price to pay. But another such enemy of conviction is ego. At the time that I was ridiculing the political pieties of the regime, I was travelling from school to school in the Tehran region presenting with my classmates a play

I'd written to honour the Islamic Revolution – an example of Sartrean bad faith if ever there was one. The play was considered a wonderful piece of work by my more-conventional teachers, replete with condemnations of the Pahlavis and exhortations to 'the people' to keep the rulers of the state ever in their hearts and prayers. It was a terrific experience, going from school to school and being feted and applauded at each, and I had no great difficulty in rationalising my hypocrisy. If I could listen to applause and be awarded golden grades for performing nonsense, then was I not subverting the regime in a particularly clever way? Having my cake and eating it, too? This was my argument to my parents, in fact; to my dad, especially. I was sixteen at this time – quite old enough to invent these rationalisations, certainly, but also old enough to accept that the rationalisations were not so different from those that the despised regime itself employed. I might have argued myself out of all genuine conviction but for the example set by certain of my teachers, particularly Mrs Azimi.

Mrs Azimi was no firebrand; but, in her quiet way, she was perhaps more effective in her subversion of the regime's lies and pieties than a host of rebels would have been. She taught history. This is a task that, even in a democracy with tested institutions and a well-established pluralist tradition, is fraught with difficulties for anyone with genuine intellectual curiosity and a passion for the truth. Teaching history in the Islamic Republic was even more of a trial. Just as modern-day primary and secondary students in Japan are offered a version of their nation's role in the Second World War that glosses over embarrassing and inconvenient events (the rape of Nanjing in China, for example, and the murder of some hundreds of thousands of Chinese and Korean civilians), so textbooks in the Islamic Republic offer a version of Iran's history that endorses the regime's take on events without reference to facts, or at least to disinterestedly agreed accounts of them.

Mrs Azimi was not about to go into battle with a lance and a sword to champion truth but, when the opportunity presented itself, she made use of other weapons to uphold objectivity: she nudged, she prodded, she gave the occasional shove. She only took such risks when she was encouraged to do so by the curiosity of the student. I was curious, and so were some of my classmates. Little by little, she lifted a veil and allowed us to see a second, unofficial drama to compare with the official one. This was thrilling. I asked questions; I was given answers. It was not Mrs Azimi herself who provided the answers; she was too wary for that. Instead, she allowed me to borrow books that had been published before the Revolution, difficult to come by, in which I was able to find the answers myself. I know, of course, that there are often no incontestable 'answers' when it comes to such questions in history as who did what, when, where, and why. But it is possible to find yourself more attracted to interpretations of events in which a greater complexity of thought is evident.

I can't say that I read Mrs Azimi's books with a perfectly open and objective mind, but at least I didn't bring to the task the mindset of an ideologue. I came to realise how likely I was to side with views that contradicted those in my high school textbooks, and I cautioned myself against exchanging one blinkered view of my nation's history for another. I would never say that I had a gift that told me when I was reading the truth but, like many another conscientious student of history, I could at least tell when one account of events was more reliable than another. In my high school textbooks, no time or space was allowed for reflection; all statements were categorical. In Mrs

Azimi's books, the authors offered their readers the opportunity to disagree. It was refreshing to see *evidence* offered to support a point-of-view. Evidence! What a beautiful concept! And again how refreshing to see self-interested testimony exposed. It was taken for granted by these writers that a statement by someone with something to gain from being believed called for scrutiny. It was as if the writers were saying to me, 'Use your brains; reflect on what you know of life; be sceptical; recognise that most people will lie for the sake of advantage; make up your mind in your own good time.'

Something I noticed again and again when comparing accounts of historical events was the sheer pettiness and ill-will of the school text versions. An example was the textbook story of the political strife in Iran in the early 1950s, when the prime minister at the time, Dr Mohammed Mossadeq, nationalised the Iranian oil industry. Mossadeq was widely admired in Iran, even after the Islamic Revolution, for having stood up to the foreign oil companies, particularly British Petroleum — so much so that the date of nationalisation was observed each year with a public holiday, even under Pahlavi (who was no friend of Mossadeq and who, in fact, denationalised the oil industry as soon as he got the chance). I grew up with not one but three versions of events: the version accepted by the general public; the version sanctioned under the reign of Pahlavi; and the version promoted by the Islamic regime after 1979 and endorsed in school texts.

The publicly accepted version was that the Shah, acting entirely at the bidding of the foreign oil companies that had installed him on the throne in 1941 after the Allied powers forced his Axis-leaning father into exile, had connived with the CIA to get rid of Mossadeq. In this version, Pahlavi repaid the Americans by delivering Standard Oil a 40-per-cent share of the denationalised oil industry, restoring the remaining 60 per cent to British Petroleum. The Pahlavi version (accepted by my father and, so far as I could see, by all those who supported the Shah's regime) was that Mossadeq had almost destroyed the oil industry by acting without regard to economic realities, such as the nation's dependence on oil income, and that only the sage intervention of the Shah had saved the nation from the disaster of bankruptcy. (In this version, it is allowed that Mossadeq loved his country, but in a misguided way.) The regime's version was that Mossadeq was a tool of British oil interests and had intended to return 100 per cent of the Iranian oil industry to them, but had been thwarted by the Pahlavi-backed CIA coup of 1953. A fourth version – the version I found in Mrs Azimi's books – endorsed the version accepted by the public, although with qualifications and caveats.

What amazed me was that the regime should have thought it necessary to discredit Mossadeq, to deny him his due as an enemy of the Pahlavis and a friend to the nation. The Pahlavis were the enemy of both Mossadeq and the mullahs, after all. Standing up to foreign interests was exactly what the regime was prepared to applaud. If there were one figure in pre-revolutionary Iran whom the regime should have lionised, wouldn't that be Mossadeq? But, no. When people put up posters of Mossadeq on Nationalisation Day, the regime's stooges tore them down or defaced them. The regime so detested Mossadeq that it contrived a highly implausible theory to explain why he had bothered to nationalise the oil industry to start with.

So I puzzled and puzzled over the regime's motives and, bit by bit, prodded by Mrs Azimi, I came to understand: the regime could not afford to concede that a secularist had done the nation a service.

At the time of reading Mrs Azimi's books, I had no way of knowing that the regime's strategy of writing the history that best suited it was employed by despots, tyrants, totalitarians, and democratically elected leaders all over the world. I had not read *Darkness at Noon*, with its portrait of the Soviet regime's thought-police. I had not studied the show trials in Nazi Germany. I had not taken enough interest in British history to discern the self-serving fictions of successive British governments on the question of Ireland. But I could see what Mrs Azimi was getting at: to the powerful, truth is negotiable.

One anomalous benefit of being educated in an Iranian secondary school is that philosophy was (and is) an elective subject in the higher levels. It was okay for philosophy teachers to nurture critical habits of thought, and the works of great thinkers from Aristotle to Sartre remained uncensored. This liberty of enquiry is partly explained by Persian custom, and partly by the philosophy that underpins Islam. Persians have honoured philosophy and philosophers since the days of the Persian empire under Darius the Great, while Islam is not in its nature inimical to daring thought. A competent Islamic scholar will find ways to accommodate the entire output of any of the great philosophers within the capacious edifice of his faith. (Non-Muslims, particularly those in the West, are usually unaware of the extraordinary suppleness of Islam.)

There was a third explanation for the freedom granted to philosophy teachers: the regime correctly judged that philosophy was harmless without contemporary examples to illustrate or support its contentions, and all illustrations were subject to scrutiny and embargo. Teachers could speak forever about the Aristotelean concept of public virtue, but were not permitted to point to anything in the society around them to illuminate the lesson, such as the very un-Aristotelean capriciousness evident in the banning of white socks. Nonetheless, the training in logic and analysis, and the sceptical habit of thought that my philosophy teachers insisted on, allowed me and my fellow students to draw our own conclusions.

Later, at university, my philosophy tutor, Mrs Ebrahimi, adopted a similar tactic to that of Mrs Azimi in order to keep out of hot water with the administration. She encouraged us to doubt and question, but she couldn't participate in debates. She would initiate a discussion, then announce that she intended to leave the classroom. When she returned, she said, she expected us all to be sitting with a wide space between us, wearing angelic expressions on our faces. So off she would go, and we would continue the argument. When she returned, we would still be sitting in a cluster and still arguing with all the passion that nineteen-year-olds bring to such debates. Next class, Mrs Ebrahimi would make the same announcement, and it would be disregarded in the same manner as on the earlier occasion. When I recall these wonderful teachers, I am moved by the sheer cunning they displayed in the service of the truth. Perhaps this is how the truth (what truth we have, that is) has survived since time immemorial: through the cunning, the deviousness, and the sheer imaginative bravado of people prepared to lie through their teeth to thwart falsehoods.

chapter thirteen

Although I can't be sure, I have the feeling that it's morning. If I happen to be sitting in my cell in a daze, as I often am, I can lose track of the last prayer call. Was it twelve hours ago? Was it ten minutes ago? Even mealtimes provide no gauge, since the food is the same whatever the time of day: olives and bread, and sometimes a strange paste, possibly containing fish or meat.

I must have been sleeping, not that I can remember. But I am experiencing the familiar, slow return of awareness that follows awakening. At first, all that I can think about is how cold and uncomfortable I am. My hand goes to my head to touch what is left of my hair. The feel of the stubble on my palm brings tears to my eyes, but it also fills me with anger, just briefly; I don't have the emotional strength to sustain the anger.

The blindfold is dropped into my cell through the little hatch. This means I'll be taken out; I'll be interrogated again. I can't think further ahead than the moment. I must have the blindfold on by the time the guard opens the door, or I will be punished. I draw my scarf over my bald head, and slip on the blindfold. If this really is morning, it will be the first time the interrogations have begun so early. I ask myself if this is a bad sign – as if there were any such thing as a good sign in this prison.

The sickness and fear develop rapidly, and by the time the door is opened I am trembling with paranoia. As on many earlier occasions, I find myself murmuring something that is both a prayer and, in a weird way, the opposite of a prayer: *They can do anything. They can do anything. They can do anything. Dear God, they can do anything . . .*

The guard grabs my arm and pulls me out of the cell.

'Where are you taking me?' I ask, even though it's a foolish question; the guard is not likely to give me any information and, in any case, where else could he possibly be taking me other than to the interrogation room? I think what I am trying to ask him is whether I am being taken to somewhere more dreadful. In my Spanish studies, I read of republican prisoners in something of the same situation as me recalling how important it was to know if they were being taken to execution. Knowing could not make any difference, and yet it was vital to know. This is how it feels to me. If I am to be shot in the back of the head, I want those few minutes of knowing. I want to say a farewell to my parents. Why should this be? My parents would never know what became of me if I were shot; they would not be told. They would never know that I said something loving. Just as at the time of marriage, burial, and coming-of-age, people crave a ritual to mark this most significant of all events, the final farewell.

The guard pushes me forward along the corridor.

'No talking,' he says.

Abruptly, I stop. I stand motionless in what I know to be the corridor. My legs won't move. Somehow, my senses tell me that we are not following the regular route to the interrogation room.

The guard nudges me, but I remain motionless. Animal instinct has paralysed me.

'Move it!' he growls.

'Where are you taking me? *Where?*'

'To a nice café,' he says, and gives a little grunt of a laugh.

The sickness I am feeling enlarges and throbs all through my stomach and chest.

'*Please!* Where are you taking me?'

He doesn't answer. He shoves me forward.

I tell myself, 'Don't move, Zarah, don't move!' But the guard whacks me hard on the shoulder, and my legs respond instinctively to avoid further pain. If I refuse to move, he will beat me; he has done it before. At the same time, the strength is draining from my limbs. Conflicting instincts are contending for the right to control my body. The guard is now dragging me, or almost dragging me. My feet attempt to keep up with the momentum of my body.

We stop. I can hear the guard opening a door. He pushes me into what I assume to be a cell somewhere or other in this city of a prison. He gets me seated on a chair. He wrenches my arms behind me and begins tying my wrists together. The same foolish instinct that made me stop in the corridor compels me to struggle against the bonds on my wrists, but the guard has no difficulty in overcoming my resistance. He is much stronger than me. I feel like a midget attempting to resist a giant.

I hear the guard's footfalls on the floor. I hear the door closing behind him. I sit stock-still, waiting for whatever is about to happen. I imagine the most appalling thing first (rape), then things that are less horrifying (a beating, torture). I recognise that my mind is attempting to prepare me. My mind can't help doing this. Since my physical strength is too paltry to help me in any way, only my mind can help me. But how does it help me to imagine these things? In what way will it make them easier to bear?

Nothing is happening. The room is silent.

I try to move, but it's not possible. Even the chair is anchored to the floor.

Dear God, what are they planning?

The only sound I can hear is the rapid hiss of my breathing.

I doubt I would be so terrified if I had been taken to the usual room, questioned by either of the interrogators I am used to. It's mad, but I begin to long for the room I am used to, for the abuse I am familiar with, for the stink of the fat man's breath that I know and abhor. Even without my realising it, my mind and body have been preparing themselves for the expected. The unexpected throws my preparations into disarray.

I wait. I strain my hearing to catch any new sound. I wriggle what muscles I can to relieve the onset of pain. Simply sitting can become excruciating.

How much time has passed with me strapped to this chair? Surely an hour? A mind, any mind, cannot endure nothingness for very long. Certainly, my mind cannot. I attempt prayer, but talking to God is unavailing when your mind is demanding concrete experience. I sniff the air, smell the mouldy stink of wet carpet left to rot. Have I been stuffed into some ancient storeroom? Has this room been chosen for its special stench – the stench we imagine we'd encounter in crypts? That would appeal to the sense of humour of the cretins who guard this place.

The bonds on my wrists are making my hands numb. I open and close my fingers to the extent that I can. Now I am becoming aware of a number of sites of discomfort all over my body. I want to rouse my shoulders and stretch them, lift my behind from the seat of the chair, raise my legs. And what will happen if I want to pee?

The immobility is acting on my brain like the screech of fingernails drawn down a blackboard.

Is it two hours now? Surely it is two hours. I'm going to say two hours, because it must be that long. It must be. Perhaps it is even longer. Perhaps I am underestimating. It could be three hours. Maybe three hours is the limit. Maybe the interrogator will come after three hours. He might slap me across the face. Well, let him. Let him do what he likes. Let him blow his filthy breath right into my nostrils. Let him curse me, call me a whore, a bitch, a traitor, whatever he likes. I will say, 'Yes, yes, I am a whore, the worst whore you can imagine, and the worst bitch, and the worst traitor! Yes, yes, yes!'

I am no longer afraid. Boredom has eroded my fear away. I think of people who have withstood solitary confinement for long, long periods – for months or even years. What sort of minds must these people have to overcome the murderous boredom? They must have extraordinary resources of character and conviction. I am not like those people. My resources are very limited. Why don't they realise, the interrogators, that my resources are limited? Why don't they just give me one really big beating and break my spirit completely, then make me do whatever they want? Because I will. I know I will. I know I don't have the courage of a martyr. I want to scream out, 'Fools! I am just a girl! If you tried, you could destroy me easily! Come and try!'

Now a suspicion grows in my mind, slowly at first: they have forgotten me. They don't remember where I am. Maybe they are looking for me even now. One guard is saying to another, 'That stupid girl, that Zarah what's-her-name, where did you put her?'

'Is anyone here?' I whisper.

There is no answer. I say again, 'Is anyone here?'

My back is beginning to hurt badly. I resent them having forgotten me. I am a prisoner here! I deserve to be watched and guarded! If I have no other rights, at least I have the right to be watched and guarded!

Where have they gone? Has something incredible happened outside the prison, making all the guards and interrogators run away? Nuclear war, something like that?

The idea of having been forgotten brings fear back – the fear that the boredom had destroyed. Or, no, this is a new fear – the fear of being thought irrelevant, completely unimportant, not worth the effort of torturing.

My neck is aching unbearably.

'Hey, is anyone here? For God's sake, I am here, in this room!'

I haven't dared to shout very loudly.

I try to compose myself, regain my wits. I tell myself, 'All you are doing is sitting in a chair for a few hours. So, big deal! Anyone can do that!'

I think of the university entrance exam, a year ago now. The exam took four hours. It was a nightmare. Every muscle in my body ached. But I survived. 'Make yourself calm, Zarah, silly Zarah,' I say aloud to myself.

Instead of thinking calming thoughts, I begin to mutter bitter rebukes to the invisible interrogators. 'What sort of interrogators are you? No beatings, no torture, just letting a person sit in a chair? You don't even know how to do your job. Just a simple job like this, probably the only job you morons can do, and even then you fail.'

I repeat these rebukes again and again, adding more detail each time. I realise that I'm veering toward madness, but I can't stop myself. All at once, I'm screaming my head off, rage and fear and disgust pouring from me in a torrent: 'I'm here, you idiot! You, whatever your name is, I'm here! Why don't you come in? I've got things to say! You don't even know a tiny bit of what I've done! I've done horrible, horrible things! Come in, you stupid bastards!'

The door opens straight away. I instantly experience a crazy delight. I made something happen! But before I can comprehend anything more, I feel tape being stuck over my mouth. Fingers smooth the tape tight, from hinge to hinge of my jawbone. Then the door slams shut again.

My ears are full of the sound of my breathing shrieking in and out through my nostrils. I can feel my chest heaving with the effort of gaining enough breath to live. In a normal, relaxed state, respiration through the nostrils is sustaining; in a state of terrified arousal, the absolute removal of the option to breathe through one's mouth is physically traumatising. It takes long minutes before my breathing is again under control. Tears of frustration wet my eyes behind the blindfold. Oh, what a clever Zarah! You can't see, you can't move, and now you find a way to make yourself mute and make breathing ten times as hard! And guess what, idiot? When they pull this tape off, your lips are going to come off with it! Idiot, idiot, idiot!

I'm so tired now. The aches and pains in my body have spread everywhere. Each muscle, hundreds of them, is pleading for relief. Even worse than the aching of my muscles is the silence. I attempt to make a sound by tapping my foot on the floor, but there is no response. Either the floor is made of something that muffles sound or I don't have the strength in my ankles to create enough force. I try again. I'm quite desperate now. Any sound would be like a huge dose of painkillers. But I can't even make the tiniest sound – just nothing. My tears are making pools of my eyes.

It has become impossible for me to judge how long I have been sitting here. Pieces of my brain and body seem to be fading. I can sense the gaps.

I have suddenly realised that I am hungry, and now it is hunger that has become my chief torment. It seems such a long time ago that I felt food in my mouth. Thinking of the taste of food makes my gorge rise, for some reason that I can't understand. Is it that I crave food so much that I am making myself sick? I try to block out the urge to vomit, but it gains strength until I can't fight it any longer. My mouth fills with vomit, but I can't eject it. I can barely breathe now. I try to swallow the vomit back down, but it returns and returns. I try to blow the vomit out through my nose, and my head fills with stink. I try again, but it's hopeless.

I am awake, still in my chair. I am sopping wet and freezing cold.

They must have thrown a bucket of water over me. I must have fainted. I can feel trickles running down the flesh of my back.

With the passing of time, the only thing I am hoping for is that an end will come. I don't mean death – just an end to what my body, both the outside of it and the inside and the stuff in my brain, is enduring. I am holding as fast as I can to the idea that things have endings. I know now that they haven't forgotten me. I know now that what I had thought of as neglect is, in fact, a form of torture. This is all that they have in mind for me today: the sitting-and-doing-nothing torture. It will have an end. They don't intend, I am sure, to make me sit here until I die of hunger or thirst or exhaustion. For all I know, it may be an experiment. Maybe they are making bets on how long I will last before I faint again. That would fit in with their mentality. They are torturers, but they like to make their job as entertaining as possible.

The pain in my body makes me moan, but the moan that comes out of me is shocking. It is not the deep, anguished moan of a woman, but that of a tiny child, almost of a baby – a weak, wispy little sound. I sound to myself like someone in a silly horror movie; like a child-wraith. But it's scary, all the same. Is this all the strength that is left in me?

Time is passing like the time in deep space. Time that goes on and on, and means nothing. Time that is never recorded on the face of a clock. Black time.

And now what?

I am being dragged. I can feel four hands on me, two on each arm. I must have fainted again. The feel of my body on the hard surface below me is strange. I am moving, but it is not me who is making the movement happen. So odd! The tape is gone and my mouth hangs slackly open. I can smell vomit, and also the denser smell of blood.

The dragging stops. I can hear a cell door being opened. Is it my cell? Happiness begins to build in the pit of my stomach. It rises into my chest. This could be my cell. This might be where they have been dragging me, to my cell, my home. Now, as I am dragged a little further, and left, and the door slams shut, I am sure. The happiness is overwhelming.

I take off my blindfold and drop it out through the slot in the door. The beauty of seeing! The wonder of it! And there *was* an end! I waited, and an end came! Dear God, thank you for endings!

The weird man in the upper cell stops moaning. 'Are you still alive?' he asks.

'Yeth,' I answer in that scary, lisping, child-wraith voice.

'It's been twelve hours and 9 minutes since they took you,' he says, and starts giggling. The giggling lasts only for a minute. Now he is moaning for Leila again.

'I'll kill you, Leila! As God is my witness! I'll kill you!'

A tray of food is pushed under the door. I can smell it from where I'm lying on my blanket. It's only a metre away from me, but a metre is too far. I can't make myself move over a distance as great as that. It's too far, too far. But the smell of the food — very ordinary stuff, just prison glug — is unbearably beautiful. I make my body do things it doesn't wish to do; I make muscles and bones move across the concrete floor. I try to grasp the spoon, but my hands are still so numb that the spoon drops from them. I try again to hold the spoon, and again with no success. My wrists and hands are a weird blue colour, nothing like the colour of human flesh. It's impossible to imagine that my hands might ever be a normal colour again. I make a very concentrated effort to hold the spoon, and this time it remains in my grasp. I heap the food into my mouth — horrible food, stale rice with a sauce that stinks like an open rubbish bin. Oh, but the taste of it! The heavenly taste of it!

⁓

I wake in the morning to the sound of Azan, the morning call to prayer in Arabic. The first thing that comes into my head is an image of six-year-old kids, many of them, sitting in front of me in my old classroom at primary school. I see myself in this image, too – even though, at the time, this could not be possible. And what am I doing? Why am I standing there in front of the class looking so sulky and resentful? I was never a sulky kid, so what is the matter with me?

I take myself back to that time, struggle for comprehension and then, without warning, the memory rises into my consciousness. This was punishment! I had been making fun of Azan or, more correctly, making fun of Arabic. All of us kids made fun of Arabic. We hated learning it, hated speaking it, and considered it unpatriotic to use the language of the stupid Arabs. In my Zoroastrian household, Arabic was held in particular contempt, for it was the language of the people who had swarmed over Persia and forced the people to their knees 800 years earlier. The resentment of that invasion and subjugation had been passed down from generation to generation for all that time. And I must have been the loudest in my protests, for in this memory I am being compelled to sing the call to prayer at the top of my voice. So there I stand, hating what I am about to do, but I do it anyway. I throw my head back and bawl out Azan:

Come, ye faithful,
Bow to God and give Him your praise
Praise the Maker of Earth
Praise the Father of the Prophet
Come, ye faithful,
Bow to God and give him your praise

I sit, running my fingers over the stubble on my head and scratching my neck. I use my finger as a pen and write messages to myself, or else just my name on my skull. How ugly I must look now! What a fright for people to see! Oh, the interrogator knew exactly what he was doing when he made me ugly in this way. He saw my vanity. He saw how much of my self-esteem was invested in maintaining myself as a Persian princess of the past. And what do I think now? *Have my looks, bastard! What do I care? What good does looking pretty do me here? What good does looking pretty ever do anyone?* Oh, but that is disingenuous. It does people a lot of good. But not in any crucial situation, and not when anything that you hope to rely on all through life is involved, like your soul and its influence over you. Oh, but I wish I had my hair back!

Overhead, the mystery man is moaning his everlasting complaint.

'Leila! Leila, you bitch! You evil bitch!'

'Hey!' I call up to him. 'Was Leila pretty?'

He stops moaning. He must be thinking.

'Yes,' he says. 'But she was a whore.'

'Did she have long hair?'

I hear the mystery man drawing a deep breath.

'She did, long and black, but she was a bitch.'

'Where did you meet her?' I have asked him this question before, more than once, sometimes idly, sometimes out of genuine interest, sometimes just to shut him up. He always says, 'None of your damned business!'

I wait while he considers his reply. He's taking his time.

'None of your damned business!' he shouts.

Why do I bother?

'Hey, listen to me,' I call out. 'Are you really here because of money? Tell me the truth!'

He doesn't answer me. He begins again to moan the name of the woman he loves and detests: the bitch, the whore, Leila.

Well, say nothing then, I think. Why should I be concerned? But, really, I do wish to know more about Leila.

My hand goes to my skull, and my fingers roam through the stubble. I write my name in capitals across my skull, from the top of one ear to the top of the other, and again, and again:

ZARAH

ZARAH

ZARAH

chapter fourteen

My mother tongue is Farsi, the ancient language of Persia and still the official language of Iran. I thank God for that. With a little more bad fortune, I and my countrymen could well have been speaking Arabic, and Farsi might have withered on the vine, as Latin has.

Everyone believes that his or her native tongue is the language spoken by the angels in heaven. That's how it should be. But Persian, Farsi, even more than other languages, truly is the first choice of the angels. Of course, my feeling for my native tongue is entwined with my love of my country. Farsi *suits* Persians. It is an outgrowth of the Persian sensibility. I have already spoken of the Persian character in regard to love and romance, but I haven't mentioned its most adorable feature: it is the language of liars. Not of cold-blooded liars — that's not what I mean; not of liars who use language as a pickpocket uses his fingers. No, I mean those who dream; those who tell stories to themselves that they believe because of the beauty of the telling; those who use words to make roses bloom in the desert where the sun has baked the soil black and red.

Farsi is kind to the impractical, the hopeless, and the helpless;

to poets and madmen. It throws out tendrils that curl around whatever they can reach, whatever will support them for the time. It draws its nourishment up through roots that have burrowed deep down for thousands of years; roots that clasp the bones of Darius and his court poets; that curl through the relics of dancing girls who smeared kohl around their eyes and perfumed their hair and made their flesh glisten with scented oils. It is not the language of the downright, of the straight-talking, of the morally fearless. Can you ever get a straight answer from a Persian? No, it's not possible because, on the way to providing it, the Persian suddenly becomes aware of a hundred more fascinating routes to the answer; and before he or she knows it, a simple 'Yes' or 'No' has become an adventure that requires a thousand words in the telling.

It was my literature teacher, Mrs Mohammadi, who helped me fall in love with Farsi. I hadn't thought before I came to know her that my native language was anything special. I spoke it, yes; it helped me get from A to B by a very roundabout road. But its beauty was hidden from me. Mrs Mohammadi had so drenched herself in the language that she had taken on its colour and shimmer. 'Listen,' she said, and began to read one of Sa'adi's prefaces from the Golestan, or Rose Garden, a famous sequence of poems:

I remember that in my youth I was passing along a street when I beheld a beauty with the radiance of the moon in her face. The season was late summer, when the fierce heat dries up the moisture of the mouth and the scorching wind boils the marrow in the bones. Through the weakness of nature, I was unable to support the power of the day's sun and was forced to seek shelter in the shade of a wall, hoping with all my heart that some passing stranger with a pitying heart would relieve the cruel thirst I suffered and cool the flames that consumed me with the balm of water. All at once from the shaded portico of a house, I beheld a bright form appear, of such beauty that the grandest eloquence should fail to sing her beauty. She came forth as the dawn that lifts the veil of night, or as the liquor of life rising from the parched earth. She held in her hand a cup of water in which she had mixed sugar and the juice of grapes. The water was perfumed with the scent of rose petals, unless it was only that I received it from her hand and breathed in a moment the aroma of her flesh. In short, I took the cup from her fair hand, and drained its fullness, and received new life. Ah, but the thirst of my heart cannot be slaked with a cup of water, nor if I should drink rivers would it lessen the least.

In Farsi, the bloom of love's revelation is much more pronounced. It is almost as if Farsi exists for this purpose, to carry into the reader's heart once and forever the sensation of cool water touching the parched tongue; of love reaching the fragile roots woven about the heart, and reviving the poetry and tenderness of life.

It was not Mrs Mohammadi's intention to politicise the teaching of Persian literature, but it wasn't possible to illuminate the beauty and subtlety and cheerful laziness of Farsi without being political. Arabic words have bullied their way into our language; and so, whenever Mrs Mohammadi came across an Arabic word that had nudged aside a Persian word, she restored the Persian word. That was a political act; a subversive act. But she never sermonised; never put Arabic in the dock. She simply said, '*This* in place of *that* better serves the poem.'

Little by little, I began to understand. It is possible to read Sa'adi's verses and prefaces a thousand times without ever being moved, for literature cannot create the joy that comes when you recognise beauty; it can only exploit what is growing in your heart. A fine teacher like Mrs Mohammadi can awaken that joy, if it is there to be awakened, and that is what she did for me and for my friends in her class. Once the thrill of the poetry had been kindled, she went on to highlight themes to help us understand why we were thrilled, and what went into being thrilled.

They relate that once, during a hunting expedition, they were preparing for Nushirwan the Just some game, as roasted meat. There was no salt, and they despatched a slave to the village to fetch some. Nushirwan said to the slave, 'See that you pay for what you take, lest it become a custom to take without paying and the village be ruined.' Said the slave, 'Oh, Master, what harm will such a small quantity cause?' Nushirwan replied, 'The origin of injustice in the world was at first small, and everyone that came added to it, until it reached the magnitude we behold today.'

Whenever possible, Mrs Mohammadi turned her light on the theme of justice and injustice in Sa'adi and Hafiz and Rumi. Once again, she offered no sermons. But she allowed us to see that the greatest things said about justice and injustice in our language stood in such strong contrast to the far pettier things said about justice and injustice and right and wrong by the mullahs, or at least by the mullahs of the regime. Was it an insult to God to wear white socks? An insult to God to speak openly of the love in your heart for another human being, a male human being, a boy? An insult to God to let the light of the sun touch the hair of your head? And was justice being served when the girl who let the sun touch her hair was pushed into a dark cell and beaten? Who could imagine Hafiz and Rumi and Sa'adi being moved to write great poetry on the subject of the girl whose hair was exposed to the sun? What would they say? 'Oh, dark clouds filled the heavens and a hail of frogs fell to earth when the young beauty uncovered her hair'?

This is the way in which great literature is at its most subversive – by allowing the reader to see what subjects, what experiences, great writing favours, and with whom poets who have mastered the language keep company. Once literature has thrilled you deeply, you cannot imagine those who created it rejoicing in injustice, employing their pens to make sonnets that celebrate hypocrisy. Who wrote the superb poetry celebrating the triumph of the Third Reich? Who will write the superb poetry celebrating the censorship code of my country's Council of Guardians? It is certainly true that highly accomplished writers are capable of revealing vile prejudices in their work, but great literature, in its nature, does not endorse the degradation of humanity, nor even of a race, caste or class.

> Do not reveal to a friend every secret that you possess. How do you know but that at some time in the future he may become your enemy? Nor inflict on your enemy every injury that is in your power, as he may someday become your friend. Tell no one the secret that you want to keep, for no one will be as careful of your secret as yourself.

Mrs Mohammadi did not tell us her secret, but she let the secret tell itself, of its own free will. When she introduced us to

Omar Khayyam, she didn't attempt to make a hero of him to us, although he was plainly a hero to her. Just the exposure to his thought was enough to make him a hero.

> Ah, make the most of what we may yet spend,
> Before we too into the dust descend;
> Dust into dust, and under dust to lie;
> Sans wine, sans song, sans singer, and – sans end!

What four lines in all of Persian poetry could more contradict the philosophy of the mullahs? No wonder they hate him! I don't mean the exhortation to drown your sorrows in wine, but the deeper message – asking us to look at life not as a rigorous preparation for a second life, a life after death, but as an end in itself. Or not entirely as an end in itself, but as a period of seeing and breathing and tasting and loving, permitted by our senses and limbs and lips, which it would be folly to abjure out of a conviction of a greater delight to follow. Khayyam is no atheist; on the contrary, he simply says that the mind and motives of God cannot be fathomed. We know that we will die, but to die without having lived? Without having rejoiced in the sunlight, the air? Without having loved?

Almost every quatrain of Omar Khayyam's subverts the dogma of the mullahs, because his poetry is the work of an enquiring mind. You can't have an enquiring mind and talk about it publicly in Iran. You can't have an enquiring mind in two-thirds of the countries of the world. Mrs Mohammadi's gift to me and my friends was to show us what our beautiful Farsi had produced when an enquiring mind went to work with it. She didn't have to make any other point. Her point was made by itself when we left the classroom with our hair (if we were female) carefully concealed.

> Oh friend, come along so that we don't mourn tomorrow's
>   sorrow
> Oh friend, come along so that we make the best of our short
>   lives
> Tomorrow, when all of us will leave this old temple as dead
>   bees
> We won't be any more or less than thousands of others in
>   hives

One day, when Mrs Mohammadi was reciting Khayyam's poetry, I wished time could halt just for a moment. Her voice and the incandescent language of Khayyam had thrust me forward in a thousand-step leap. I wanted time to stop so that I could write something myself, something Khayyam-like, and show it to this beloved woman and win some approval from her. (Yes, I have always and forever sought what I have come to speak of in Australia as 'elephant stamps'.) Not on that day, but on other days, I showed Mrs Mohammadi whatever I wrote. Sometimes her face bloomed like a flower as she read; sometimes she frowned; sometimes she giggled.

I think of myself as a Persian rather than as an Iranian. This is not hair-splitting. Persia existed before Iran, a name for the country that only dates back to 1934, when the Pahlavis changed it to Iran, meaning 'Aryan', to impress Western powers with Persia's supposed 'white' racial pedigree. To think of myself as Persian allows me to embrace the whole of my country's history, going back to the flowering of a distinctly Persian sensibility under the early Persian emperors Achemenes, Cyrus, and Darius 2500 years ago. For the first 1500 years of Persia's existence, Zoroastrianism was the state religion; and so, by embracing Persia's past, I also embrace the roots of my religion. This may sound quasi-mystical or maybe even sentimental, but I do believe that the whole of what it means to be born in Iran can only really be enjoyed when the whole of Persia's history is in one's veins.

The ancient language of Persia, Farsi, still expresses the Persia of the past as well as the present. Reefs of gold run through the language. I don't believe that the Arab invasions of Persia between 767 and 1050, and the establishment of Islam in my ancient country, destroyed the Persian sensibility; no, up until the triumph of fundamentalism in Iran in 1979, the spiritual beauty of Islam co-existed with the beauty that prevailed before the coming of Islam. In schools, Persian history was taught without distortion – unlike in post-revolutionary Iran, where the mullahs seem to hold the pre-Islamic era in contempt. And from what I can tell, relying on what some of my teachers and my father and mother report, the intrusion of Arabic words into Farsi was not nearly so resented in the era of spiritual co-existence.

The child I have in the future, that boy or girl, or those boys and girls (even better!) must speak Farsi. English, yes; French, maybe; Italian, Spanish, perhaps. But Farsi, above all. I want to become the Mrs Mohammadi of my children's lives. I want my children to read Sa'adi and Hafiz and Khayyam and Rumi and, of course, all of those Iranian writers who are alive now. Then I want them to read the Code of the Council of Guardians of the regime. I want them to say to me, 'Mum, why has the Council of Guardians squandered such a beautiful language on this nonsense?'

chapter fifteen

'Are you really here for something to do with money?' I ask the madman, directing my voice to the fan grille. We have been chatting in a desultory way for a half-hour, and it just seems weird to me that the madman is here for theft or embezzlement or passing false cheques, while I am here for shouting in the street. My mind is an orderly one; I always grow uncomfortable with the ill-sorted, with things out of their proper categories. I know that the prison includes murderers in its population, and I can see how, to the regime, killers and political protestors are all of the one bad breed. But people like the madman who have done something peculiar with cheques? No, that I can't accept. The madman belongs in a different prison; a prison for those who transgressed without raising their voices or their fists.

I repeat my question to the madman.

The madman doesn't answer.

'What's your name? You can tell me your name, surely?'

Part of my curiosity about the madman is to do with trying to glimpse what I myself will become in the future. If you are kept here for a long time, is this what becomes of you? Do you begin to howl day and night, and rain abuse down on the heads of your loved ones? In a year or five years, will I be the madwoman in the cell above some newcomer, abusing the guards for the sake of the pitiable intimacy of a beating?

'Sohrab, it's my name,' says the madman, and I am so shocked at receiving an answer that I ask him to repeat what he has just said.

'Sohrab,' he says quietly. He has done this before, switching from pure craziness to quiet courtesy in the space of a minute. I know that I must take advantage of his sane self before it is lost in shrieking again.

'Sohrab, how long you have been here, Sohrab? How long?'

'I've lost count. Maybe seven years, eight, maybe ten. It's difficult to keep count.'

I mutter my amazement, and Sohrab laughs. It is not his madman's laugh. It is the rueful laugh of someone noticing the impact of his experience on another, far more naive person.

'Ten years?' I ask him, just to make sure I heard right.

'Ten, maybe. But maybe not ten. Maybe seven, eight. I don't know.'

This is weird. As the madman becomes quieter, more reasonable, I become crazier. Because I cannot imagine what will be left of me if I have to stay here for ten years. I will have no teeth, because I will tear them from my face in desperation. I will have no hair, because when it grows back I will rip it out again.

'Oh, God! Ten years!' I wail. 'Ten years!'

'Shush!' says the madman. 'Don't yell. If you yell, they will come and rape you. They raped Miriam; she was in your cell before you. I could hear them. Don't yell, silly girl!'

But I can't stop. The two words 'Ten years' have taken over my brain, my lungs, my throat, my mouth. I wail them out and wail and wail. Even as I wail I know I am hysterical, that I am sick. But the words won't stop.

'Shush! Stop! Stop!' says Sohrab, more urgently. 'Stop it now!'

And I do. The words grow duller on my tongue. The wail becomes a whisper.

'Ten years, please no, please no ...'

'That's better,' says Sohrab the madman, and both of us fall silent.

—

The guard drops the blindfold in through the slot, and it falls almost soundlessly to the floor. I immediately stop worrying about the future, and start thinking about what is waiting for me in the interrogation room today.

I'm like a trained rat. I have become completely conditioned by the experiments being conducted on me. A piece of fabric appears through the door and the expected reaction commences. I'm trained. And I'm tame. Trained and tame. There is not a vestige of spirit left in me. The experiment is successful, bastards. Leave me be. What more can they possibly have to ask me? They know more about me than I know about myself. Give me a piece of paper to sign, I will sign it. Whatever you like. I won't even read it, I'll just sign.

I walk stutteringly into the interrogation room, blind as usual. Every time I enter this room I picture myself looking so timid and miserable, and I picture my interrogator smiling in satisfaction. He likes the way I look. He likes what I have become. It's an endorsement of his craft, of his skill. Probably his satisfaction is more that of the proud professional than that of the sadist.

He nudges me to the chair. I sit and take a deep breath. The feel of the chair forming its shape around me makes me break out in a fit of shivering. More trained-rat responses. If I ever get out of here, it will be ages before I am able to sit upright in a chair of this sort without its associations making me ill.

This is the stinky guy; the fat, unwashed one. His smell is as distinctive as his voice.

'Where were we?' he asks himself in a business-like way. I hear him moving papers about. Now he clears his throat.

'Were you being supported by any anti-government organisations overseas?'

Hasn't he asked this question before? If so, what was my answer then? Yes? No? So far as the truth goes, I would have had to have answered, 'No'. The idea is ludicrous. We had no money, no support, no assistance at all. If one of us were beaten up by the Basijis, was there ever any money to pay the hospital bills? Not a single rial. We were like an amateur club of hobbyists. Our hobby was politics. We were passionate about it, but so are the people who make model aeroplanes or play chess. Who would give us money? Who would bother?

'No, nobody supported us.'

'You don't say. And did Arash Hazrati have any friends or connections with Iranian TV channels in L.A., or radio stations in London?'

The sense of humour people have is so fugitive, so prepared to hide itself until the chance comes to smile. He didn't say, 'Los Angeles'; he said 'L.A.'. It strikes me as very funny. But I don't smile. I will save this smile for later. And, in any case, as if any of us would watch the channels he's talking about. Those channels are shit – Iranians overseas encouraging those of us still in Iran to run out into the streets and to smash the government. Oh, sure. If they cared so much, they would be in Tehran doing exactly what they want us to do; but, no, it's so much more pleasant to make money in America and England, and give a little bit of it to people who run the TV channels. They call themselves 'The True Persians'. They are as bad as the regime itself. And if they had the chance, they would be doing exactly what the regime is doing: throwing people into jail. 'Go on, kids! Get your brains bashed in! We love you!' Maybe this is a little too harsh and, yes, I suppose it's also unfair, but I am not in the mood to be fair to those people. I never watched that rubbish. No one I knew ever watched it.

'No, none of us watched those channels. Not ever.'

'Fascinating. Has anyone ever contacted you or Arash Hazrati to make an interview or to get any information? Were you giving any information to newspapers?'

Interviews? I feel like asking this fat, stinky idiot if he is on drugs. Interviews? Who on earth would interview me? Who would care? I am the smallest fish in a school of very small fish. Nobody took any interest in us. Does he think I had some sort of celebrity status? I was nothing. We were all nothing. And what would be the sense of interviewing one of us? We were all in it together. There were no leaders.

'No, never.'

'Indeed. And would you do it if you were asked?'

'I wouldn't have anything to say.'

'What about later, if we let you go? Would you have things to say then?'

Is he serious about the possibility of letting me go? Or is he just tormenting me? If he would just take off the blindfold, I would put on a lovely performance for him. I'd open my eyes wide and say, 'Oh, no. I'd never dream of doing a thing like that! I promise!'

'No, I would have nothing to say.'

'You know, if you do,' he says, 'I will welcome you back here. And there will be a big reception for you. A lovely reception. You know what I mean, don't you?'

'Yes.'

'Another question. Did you accept any financial help from anyone during your activities?'

I did, actually. I accepted financial help from my regime-supporting boyfriend. But I can't say that.

'No. We had no expenses. We didn't need money.' In fact, sometimes we had to hire buses or pay for things that we needed for our rallies. We normally pooled what little money we had, but that wasn't always enough. Behnam helped us buy new items for the office, such as our fax machine and a computer. That was his version of solidarity – running with the hares and hunting with the hounds, as I've said. But even so, our expenses were trivial. It wasn't as if we dined in expensive restaurants discussing what we were going to do at our rallies. We were students. We were used to getting by on next to nothing. Student protest was just an extension of normal student life.

'What about Arash?' the interrogator asks. 'Did he provide money? Did he use his personal staff to help organise your nonsense?'

Ah, this is what I had feared – the whole Arash subject. They know very well that he is the one who matters; not because he is in charge, because he isn't, but because of his courage, his persistence. They home in on courage, these regime people, like sharks homing in on the smell of blood in the water. It maddens them. In the small sphere in which they operate, they know everything. Stubbornness probably means very little to them;

stubbornness can be eroded over time. Being a smart aleck doesn't mean all that much to them; wiping smiles off the faces of smart alecks is their bread and butter. But courage, real courage — that torments them.

I knew that they had offered Arash the opportunity to go to America to live and work, just to get rid of him — to buy him off, in a way. If he had accepted their offer, and then complained about the regime from America, they knew that his complaints would have had no credibility in Iran. He would have become like the people who run the anti-regime channels — apartment-house protestors. But Arash said no.

'I don't know. He never talks about his personal staff. He never speaks about anything personal.'

'Is that so? What about going to his house? Wasn't that personal?'

I make no answer. For a time, I hear nothing. Then, confirming what I dread, I hear the interrogator leaving his seat and moving closer to me.

'That was very personal, wasn't it?' he says.

I have a sickening sense that he intends to take my interrogation in a direction I don't want to contemplate. The only possible preparation is to renew the licence I have given myself to beg, to grovel. I am ready to beg, ready to grovel.

I hear the interrogator shuffling around me, circling me. He circles me more than three times, so far as I can gauge. His garments brush against my shoulders in each circuit. On his final circuit, he stops directly before me, takes my knees in his hands, and squeezes his thumbs into the flesh above the bone. I wince, but don't cry out. I sense that any shriek of pain will act on him like a spur. He is making a seething sound, like someone imitating the noise of a steam train, except that the seething is broken by short grunts. He moves behind me, takes the flesh of my neck on each side, and twists. I am baring my teeth in the effort not to scream. My face is bathed in the reek of his breath as he bends down to speak into my ear. He keeps hold of the flesh on my neck, twisting as he speaks. In a rising and falling whisper, he tells me of what he has inflicted on other victims, on other women, giving their names, each name repeated and drawn out. He tells me of their hopeless attempts at suicide; he imitates their screams.

He gathers up the flesh of my lower back through my tunic and twists. If it were not for the pain, I would scream. It is the pain that keeps my teeth clenched. As his chanting goes on, his spittle wetting the inside of my ear, I realise something that I must have been groping towards for weeks: I am the beginning and the end of what interests him; not any information I can provide, just my screams, my pleas. In my Spanish studies, I read of the practice of the Incas of Peru when they took captive a high-born enemy. They would cage the man or woman and crush a bone each day, starting at the feet and working up the body, harvesting screams for months.

I shriek at last and throw myself forward. The interrogator has hold of my arms at the elbows. I throw myself about as furiously as I can, but he is extraordinarily strong. He forces one of my elbows against the back of the chair with his knee, freeing one hand to brace my head against his mouth. The chanting is coarsened by the effort he is expending, but it goes on and on – another name, another name.

Finally he releases me, so suddenly that I crash from the chair to the floor. My shrieking has brought on a fit of coughing. I struggle to my knees, and labour to catch my breath. Inside me, when the coughing fit subsides, there is nothing but a loathing for life, for all life, for my own, for everyone's. I don't want to be part of anything living.

The interrogator has no more to say. I hear him cross the floor and take a seat at his desk. He calls for the guard, as he always does when it is time for me to be taken back to my cell.

Some time later, I am back in my cell. I know I will not be disturbed for the time being. It is their way. They finish, they begin to work on someone else, they don't even think of you until the next interrogation.

I am struggling to understand exactly what it is I feel. I make very sure I don't think of the details of what has happened. I just want to know what I feel. But it seems I have no feelings to discover. I am not in pain, but I wish to die. I don't want to die in a gradual way, not even over a period of minutes; I want to die immediately. In all truth, I can't even say it is death that I wish for. Death is simply the closest thing to it. I wish not to have a life.

With appalling timing, the madman above me, Sohrab, welcomes me back and asks in a sardonic way if I had fun. I scream at him, tell him to go to hell. He becomes quiet immediately. He doesn't even moan.

I want to wash my body, but there is no water.

Will I ever get rid of the smell of that repulsive man from my nostrils?

My feelings are returning. A type of wildness has invaded me. I could kill someone right now.

I put the green paper out to go to the toilet. Half an hour later, the guard drops the blindfold in. I pray for an argument or a

136

fight with the guard. I want him to fight with me so I can scream.

'I think you people are all sick and disgusting!' I shriek as the guard pushes me along. It's unthinkable to say such a thing. For a second or two, the guard doesn't respond at all, as if he can't believe my temerity. But then he pushes me forward so violently that I fall over. Curled on the concrete floor of the corridor, I scream out my abuse. The guard kicks me where I lie. I shield my head and stomach from his boots, but I keep swearing and cursing at him. The kicking hurts, well and truly, but at the same time it gives me a wretched relief. Perhaps it's psychotic, what I am doing; I don't know. But the fury that boils in my brain is somehow served by having enraged this guard. It feels good.

Another guard, a woman – by the sound of her cries – has come to stop the beating. She helps me to my feet.

'Why wouldn't you just shut up?' she whispers.

When we reach the toilet, I tear off my blindfold and begin howling – all of my hatred and fury and disgust with the interrogator, and disgust with myself, channelling itself into this fit.

What have I done to myself? What have I done!

My tears begin to die away. I am staring at the back of the toilet door. This is where messages are left for prisoners by other prisoners. They remain only for a short time before the guards scrape them away. I am staring at a message to me, a message from Arash. I know it is from Arash because the message takes the form of lines from a famous poem; lines that Arash often recites before giving a speech. The fact that the lines are scratched here means that Arash is now in Evin himself. This is no shock to me; it had become obvious that he would be arrested soon.

The lines come from a poem about love. The voice in the poem comforts a woman whose heart is aching: 'You will fly your birds soon and a kind hand will hold your empty hand.' I snort in disgust once I've read the lines. What on earth is he trying to tell me? Actually, I don't want to know. Half of what has happened to me is because of him, and the other half is because I'm a woman. I have brought my spoon with me, secretly kept back when I returned my food tray in case I ever wished to leave a message here. I use the end of the spoon handle to write below his message, 'My bird's wings are broken'. This is my message to him. I have no interest in the wings of birds at this time. I replace my blindfold, conceal my spoon, and go back to my cell.

The pain I could not feel earlier is now all that I can feel. The pain in my body accompanies the pain in my heart and my soul at each throb.

I keep thinking about Arash's message, against my will. I happen to know that the poet himself was a protestor, and that he spent years in jail. But what on earth is in Arash's head? Is he trying to give me hope? Is that what he means? If that was his plan, then it's been a complete failure. I don't feel stronger in the slightest.

I have lost everything here. That is the truth. I will never let birds fly again, not even ugly, stupid, screeching birds. Not now.

It's been a few days with no interrogation.

I go about my business, such as it is. I was permitted to have a shower yesterday. I washed my prison clothes. Thrilling.

But something is wrong in my head. My anger and sadness have withered away. What I think of now is murder. I think of it all the time: murder. When I sleep, I dream about murder. But the murders are not so triumphant in my dreams as they are in my waking life. I murder the interrogator in my dreams, but the blows I inflict don't kill him. He collapses and seems good and dead, but then he sits up and smiles. I know what this is all about, of course. I've read Freud in my philosophy classes. These are dreams of impotence. Okay, but just give me a knife or a hammer and put me in a room with that vile man, and impotence won't be a concern. Not for a moment.

And yet it distresses me to be turning homicide over and over in my brain. This is the sort of corruption that violence breeds in its victims. Do I really want this? Do I want the interrogator to have succeeded so completely that he can twist my mind out of shape and make me relish what I have always been sickened by? Or maybe this is simply a type of therapy that my imagination is administering. Fantasies of revenge. Fantasies of power.

I have been reading the Koran for the last two days. One passage reads, 'Respect your women even when they are walking past you in the street because they are God's gift to the earth, to give birth and make you happy.'

I want my Islamic rights.

—

There's a noise at my door. No blindfold has been dropped through the slot, but someone is about to enter. I am instantly hysterical with fear. The door is swung open, and there stands the interrogator, the man I have been putting to death over and over; the man who screams for mercy after I have struck him to the floor and stood above him with my knife raised.

He is not alone. A man in a doctor's white coat stands a little behind him. But no guard.

'Hello, sister. How are you today?' the interrogator asks mildly, as if this is his normal tone in addressing me. 'This gentleman is a doctor. He's here for an inspection.'

The interrogator looks straight at me without the faintest suggestion of shame. He knows that I could tell the doctor what he did to me; but he knows, too, that I won't. Such an accusation would be meaningless in this place. They execute people here every morning of the week. I know from the whispers outside Evin that the methods of torture at the disposal of men like the interrogator go as far as torture can possibly go. What complaints of inhuman abuse were made by the inmates of Nazi death camps as they waited for the end? Did those poor, wretched people believe that any protest they might make could change their fate?

'Do you have any health problems?' the doctor asks politely. 'Any pain? Do you feel sick?'

'No,' I reply. 'I'm fine.'

The interrogator smiles at me. It is a practised smile, perfectly judged for its effect. It is meant to satisfy the feelings of the doctor, in case the doctor should believe that the interrogator is just a regular guy going about his rounds; but, at the same time, the smile acts as an instrument of torture on me – a more effective instrument than a gloating laugh.

The doctor does a quick check: eyes, mouth, pulse. He records the results of this conscientious examination on a form.

When the doctor and the interrogator leave, the man I yearn to kill smiles at me and says, 'Thank you, sister, for your time.'

'Have you ever been inspected by any doctor?' I ask the madman, Sohrab, a little later.

The madman laughs. I'm so exhausted by his laughter and his craziness, but who else is there to talk to?

'Yes,' he says. 'Always say that you are good, otherwise Gholamreza will get angry.'

'Why do they send a doctor?' I ask him. 'Why do they bother?'

'To show that they care,' says Sohrab.

This is beyond belief, but I am laughing. And Sohrab joins in with my laughter. Here are the two of us: one a madman with a brain so abused that he doesn't even know how many years have passed since he was anything other than a prisoner of Evin; the other, a madwoman keeping herself alive on bloodthirsty fantasies. And both of us are laughing.

'Heaven forbid you should get ill in here!' says Sohrab, and our laughter renews itself.

'How do you know his name?' I ask Sohrab.

'You find out a lot of things when you live here,' he replies.

Oh, that cuts deep! *When you live here.* That's what the madman accepts – that this is his only home, his only address. But I haven't accepted that yet. I don't live here. Unless it's true.

'Have you ever had any visitors?' I ask.

'I did at the end of the first year. My mum. She had a heart attack a week after seeing me, and they told me that she was dead. I refused to see anyone else after that.'

'Did you cry? Did you miss her?'

'No, I was happy because she didn't have to wait for me and suffer anymore.'

'I don't want my mum to die.'

'No one does.'

He is right. No one does.

I feel sorry for Sohrab; deeply sorry. It is maternal, such a strange thing. Perhaps it was the news of his mother dying of a heart attack all those years ago that has aroused this odd, protective instinct in me. I don't know.

'Do you want me to tell a story?' I ask him. 'You might fall asleep.'

'Story, what story? I don't want to sleep. Tell me a story if you want to. I will listen. But it would be better if you could sing. I like singing.'

'I don't sing all that well. What song would you like me to sing?'

'Do you know that new song, the one about the girl singing to her doll? Do you know that one?'

I'm shocked. The pop song he is talking about came out years and years ago. But he thinks it is new. Maybe he has been here much longer than he knows? I don't tell him this, however. I don't want to upset him.

My baby doll, it's bed time,

It's bedtime and you must sleep now,

I will sing about your pretty eyes even when they close,

You must sleep now, my baby doll,

I don't want you to see that I'm crazy in love with a doll,

So you must sleep now, you must sleep.

I can't go on with the song. Its foolish innocence makes me weep.

'Don't cry,' says the madman. 'Why would you let yourself cry? You'll just become thirsty, and they won't give you any water to help.'

'Oh God, oh God! I don't want to be here!'

'No one does, but you'll be gone soon.'

'How do you know?' I say scornfully. 'What does "soon" mean to you? You don't even know how long you've been here. "Soon" could be ten years to you. It could be a hundred years!'

I shouldn't have said that. I repent instantly. I can't tell if Sohrab has taken offence, since he is silent. Then, just when I am beginning to feel that my despair has chased away the only voice that I can rely on, the madman asks me a question.

'Did you kill someone?'

'No,' I answer, quite startled, for it is as if my fantasies of murder have seeped out of my brain like a colourless gas and drifted up through the fan grille into Sohrab's cell.

'Why do you ask me that? Do I sound like I murder people?'

'I did,' says Sohrab. 'My boss. Years ago.'

I am shocked to hear this. Or no, it isn't true to say I am shocked. I am surprised, but more fascinated than anything. My pet madman is a killer? I have a new-found sense of solidarity with killers, or with killers of a certain sort. My fascination is to do with a hope that the victim of my lovely madman's crime was a prison guard – or, even better, an interrogator. But knowing what I wish to hear jolts me. My hunger for revenge is right out of control. Here I am, listening to a lunatic telling of his crimes as a spur to my own sick appetites. I shouldn't go on listening. I shouldn't encourage him to tell me anything more. But I do.

'Is that why they brought you here? Not because of a bad cheque, but because you killed someone?'

'No.'

My madman doesn't volunteer anything further, and I become impatient.

'Tell me!' I demand.

'Will I tell you?'

'Yes. Tell me.'

He is silent for long minutes. I begin to feel that I would slap him and beat him and make him tell me if I could walk into his cell.

'I will tell you,' he said. 'You sang for me.'

And he tells me his story in a completely matter-of-fact way. I am enthralled from his first sentence. I don't even question the truth of what he is saying. I believe him. If his story is all lies, at least it is entertaining. But in my heart, if not my brain, I don't believe he is making up a single thing. Whatever he is, he is not a man who makes up stories. I think he is telling the truth, so far as he can judge.

The madman, my lovely madman, my beautiful, mad friend, tells me that he was a surgeon. He worked, so he says, in Imam Khomeini Hospital; and, when he says this, there is no hint of irony in his tone. It was at the hospital that he met the famous Leila, the woman who so haunts his days and nights. Leila was his very beautiful patient. The madman fell in love with her instantly.

'You fell in love with your own patient?' I gasp.

'Yes. Are you ashamed of me?'

'No,' I answer. 'But you were a particularly naughty doctor.'

He laughs in delight at this. It is a different laugh altogether than his normal laugh, which is so tinged with sarcasm. I laugh along with him. I can't explain why in any intelligent way; but, despite everything, even what was done to me a few days ago, I am happy. How can this possibly be? I am happy. I know it is a small space of happiness, a niche, but I hold it in my heart thankfully. Oh, you beautiful madman, I think. You beautiful, disgraceful, scandalous madman!

Within two months of meeting Leila, my madman was married to her. He adored her; she adored him. Also, she was pregnant.

'You certainly didn't waste any time,' I say.

'This was love,' he replies, and there is just a faint note of chiding in his words.

'Yes, I understand.'

'It was all good. All romantic and loving. Too good to be true.'

He stops for a time. Oh, please, please keep going! I exhort him, although without saying anything aloud. I sense that levity is no longer going to please him, and I must judge anything I say carefully. This is my madman's great story; the story that keeps him alive – love, betrayal, fantasies of revenge. I mustn't bruise him.

'Then what?' I urge him, once his silence has gone on for too long. 'Any kids? Where did you go for your honeymoon?'

'No honeymoon. She was pregnant, remember. We couldn't travel because she wasn't feeling well.'

'Oh, such a shame. Then what? What happened?'

'I got a big promotion. I was hired by a big shot in the health system. A boss. Big administrator.'

'Wow, did you? You must have been good.'

He falls silent again. Oh God, surely he didn't take what I said the wrong way? I was being sincere, not satirical! But then he speaks again, and I am relieved. 'Yes, I was good. Evin is heaven. Only the very best come here.'

We laugh together. It's okay, I haven't upset him. His sense of humour is stronger than I judged.

He goes on to explain, my madman, that he was so good that the big-shot administrator had to get rid of him. He'd stumbled on evidence that the administrator was helping himself to money from the departmental budget – very large sums of money. It worried him, the thefts, and he questioned his boss, but was told that it wasn't his job to study accounts. He persisted because it distressed him; corruption of that sort always made him feel ill, he said. It was, after all, money that was supposed to be used to provide medical care for people. He probed deeper, in secret, and came to the conclusion that the big sums of money that regularly went missing were going to overseas accounts.

'But what did this have to do with Leila? How did she become your enemy?'

'They made false documents to show that I had a drug addiction and to prove that I wasn't competent to be a surgeon. I was sacked, but I had to prove them wrong, at least to my wife. I didn't want to lose her. I broke into the office one night to collect what I needed to take to the court, but I got arrested by security – and the rest is history.'

'You haven't told me what made you hate Leila.'

'She swore in court that she'd seen me taking drugs, and she said I was violent and that I'd threatened to kill her if she ever told anyone.'

'But she loved you, didn't she? You said she did.'

'I saw her in the court for the last time. She was sitting next to my boss and laughing with him. Did I tell you that she had a dimple on her cheek?'

'Yes, you told me.' About a hundred times, in fact. 'When did you kill him?'

'I tried to kill myself, but it didn't work out. I ruined it. They took me to Ghasr in Tehran, the hospital for crazy people. I ran away in the afternoon and killed him the same night. I couldn't find Leila.'

'Did you feel any better after killing him?' This was something I wanted to know.

'I did, but I would have felt even better if I could have killed Leila, too.'

'But you loved her. You said you loved her. You wouldn't have killed her. Even if you'd found her, you wouldn't have killed her.'

'Yes,' he says, 'I would have killed her. She ruined my life. So long as she is alive, she will ruin lives.'

I have to think about that. I don't ask him any questions for the time being, and he falls silent, my madman. I think about justifications for murder. I don't believe that Sohrab had the right to murder Leila, even if he'd found her that night, but I think I have the right to murder the man I despise. What will he ever contribute to the human race? He exists to make misery. I can kill a person like that.

But it is too much to tease out the full argument of justification. I'm not in court. I just want to murder someone who wouldn't even be missed by his mother. I'd settle for that.

chapter sixteen

If my mother's vision of the perfect life for a family were painted on canvas, the portrait would show a father and mother hemmed in by a half-dozen smiling children standing before a cottage overgrown with roses. The father would be attempting to look both stern and a little remote, as if the affairs of the world weighed on him heavily. But this same father would not be able to conceal his great pride in his children; it would show in his eyes. The mother would be helpless to display anything other than the joy of being surrounded by the six most physically beautiful and spiritually refined children to be found anywhere on earth, ever. The children themselves would be holding hands, as if to demonstrate their inexhaustible affection for each other. A golden radiance would hover over the family, suggesting a type of blessedness, for this family has been smiled upon by the Almighty.

My mother knew that her vision would never be realised all by itself; she knew she would have to roll up her sleeves and make it happen. She worked day and night to nurture its elements. If my elder brother found a wicked pleasure in punching me on the arm until I bruised, then denying that he had been within a kilometre of me all day, my mother would dismiss his protestations and force him to embrace me, look me in the eyes, and tell me that he loved me with all his heart. If my sisters annoyed me enough to make me hiss at them, I would be required to smile at them for a lengthy period (through gritted teeth, however). When we went on camping holidays in the forest, Mum had us all holding hands and singing songs over our nightcaps of hot chocolate. My father was compelled to heap extravagant praise on our artwork, my brothers and sisters had to gather around and all but sing with glee whenever I brought home a prize from school, and each member of the family had to give evidence, each day, of his or her delight and gratitude at being part of this radiant family.

And my family was, in fact, as lovely as it pretended to be. My mother created us in the image of her ideal; she succeeded. We did indeed love each other. My father adored each of us and found some special way of showing it; in my case, as I've said, by brushing my hair as I sat on his lap and crooning sweet songs into my ear. Of course, a family created in this way has to turn a blind eye to a great deal of what is going on around it. And both of my parents were very accomplished turners of the blind eye.

Let me explain.

My father was a senior army officer in the latter years of the Shah's reign. He was well-informed, and would have known a great deal about the rough-and-tumble (sometimes the very bloody rough-and-tumble) of Iranian politics. The contending forces in Iranian politics over the period of my father's appointment included the communists; a disenfranchised clergy; liberal and social-democratic parliamentarians; and arch-conservative nationalists. Of these groups, the communists and the disenfranchised clergy were the most volatile. The Shah detested the communists as the natural enemies of his class, and as the avowed enemies of the United States, his principal backer amongst world powers. (The CIA put him on the throne, after all.) The Shah's antagonism toward the clergy was even more personal; there has never been a formally legislated division of church and state in Iran, only a de facto division, ramped up steadily by the Shah from the beginning of his reign. Despising communists is one thing – everybody in Islamic Iran other than the communists themselves despised them, atheists that they were – but despising the clergy, and finding ways, year-by-year, to erode their power and influence, reflected the Shah's ambition for a semi-secular Iran to take its place amongst the more sophisticated nations of the world.

The Iranian clergy was amongst Iran's biggest landowners, but its lands were the chief target of the Shah's land reforms of the 1960s. This might have won him some popular praise, but it didn't, since it was well noted that the land for land reforms and redistribution did not come from the vast holdings of Pahlavi's wealthy backers. In any case, the great majority of Iranians are Muslims before almost anything else. The Shah was never a popular figure; he was always seen as an American stooge with a very tenuous claim to the Peacock Throne. Enraging the clergy was never going to strengthen his hold on power. Out in the countryside, where most Iranians lived, the mullahs planted seeds of hatred for Pahlavi, and they watered the ground assiduously. The rest of the world may have been baffled at the reception Ruhollah Khomeini received when he returned to Iran in 1979, but anyone with a basic grasp of Iranian politics would have anticipated the rapture.

The Shah could not rely on the love of the people to remain on the throne, either; he relied instead on a highly effective secret police force and on the security agency, SAVAK. The Shah's agents spent most of his reign grabbing political enemies off the streets and bustling them into prison. Files and records seized after the Shah's downfall revealed the extent of surveillance during his reign and just how widespread the summary arrests and executions were. Details of interrogation were also revealed, including methods of torture. Skilled tormentors of medieval times would not have exceeded the torturers of SAVAK in their cruelty and barbarity. The worst things that can be inflicted on the human body were inflicted in my country under the rule of the Shah.

What I have learned about the Iran of my parents I learned from sources outside my family. My father was capable of criticising the Pahlavis, but not with any great gusto. He didn't know the worst of what was being done, and neither did the Shah. Of course, the Shah's ignorance was policy; my father's was, I would guess, much more genuine.

Can I say this without dissembling? Can I claim that my father's tales of his time in the Shah's employ were truthful, so far as he knew the truth? I know perfectly well that the world is used to stories of sons and daughters passionately disputing the reputed involvement of their fathers in shocking episodes of murder and torture. I know that these sons and daughters are often blinded by loyalty, unable or unwilling to look at the facts objectively. I know that sons and daughters who have experienced only one version of the suspected or accused parent – often a reformed version – find it impossible to believe that a second, more sinister, version rounded up Armenians or Czechs or Poles or Greeks or Jews of a dozen nationalities or Vietnamese villagers or Iraqi villagers, and watched them die. I know that scepticism is justified. But when it would have been a simple thing for him to flee, after the fall of the regime he supported, my father chose to remain in Iran.

Within two weeks of Khomeini's triumph, the Ayatollah's supporters were working through a prepared list of enemies – a very long prepared list – and lynching those enemies in sheds and warehouses and on the streets of cities. Many were carted off to be subjected to the very torments they had sanctioned while in power. My father's name was not on that list. Later, when squads of zealots combed villages, towns, and cities throughout the length and breadth of the country sniffing out second-level and third-level Pahlavi supporters, my father was not a target. Basijis came to our suburb in Tehran and conducted an ad hoc investigation of people who had served the Shah in any capacity whatsoever, arresting anyone with a tang of complicity about him, closely questioning the neighbours of people they suspected for hints and suggestions, conducting a modern-day auto-da-fé – but they had nothing to complain of when it came to my father's service to the Pahlavis. He had served his country loyally, and was unapologetic about having done so. He was let be.

And yet it is probably true that my father knew that certain very unwholesome agencies existed to deal with dissenters. He would have heard things; he would have noticed things. He might have accepted the repression of the communists without too much angst, but I doubt that he would have approved at all of the way the clergy was abused – he is, after all, a man of faith. Although I have said that both of my parents were capable of turning a blind eye when they chose to, I meant only that they were blandly negligent in the way that we all are. I wouldn't suggest that my father turned a blind eye in the direction of SAVAK. I have read of certain German army officers in the Second World War returning from business in the east of the country, and even further east, in other countries, conquered countries, who were never quite the same again. What they had seen they wished they could un-see. Did my father have an experience of this sort? I don't think so. It would be more in keeping with his character for him to have simply refused to pry. But whatever the facts, I didn't accept either my father or my mother as a reliable witness to the Shah's regime once I was old enough to ask questions.

My family had lived a privileged life, it's true. So when my father returned to civilian life and established his small electronics business in the bazaar, we were unprepared for a diminished standard of living. The Iraqis attacked and the bombs fell, and my family was as much in danger as any other. The food shortages, the rationing, the squalor – it wrenched us just as it wrenched millions of other Iranians. But, unlike most Iranians, we had something to look back on, in a wistful way. We hadn't been amongst the millions whom the Shah had ignored; those who had largely gone without medicine because they couldn't afford it, and without basic social services because any welfare there was had to be spread amongst far too many of the desperately needy. And so, with a past of privilege to mourn, my father and mother began to imagine things.

Let me go forward from the war years of the 1980s to the middle of the next decade. I am now fifteen, sixteen. The Islamic Revolution has survived the war with Iraq, and has consolidated itself all over Iran. My parents may have hoped that the mullahs would just go away, but the mullahs have waited for thirty years to rule Iran, and they intend to go on ruling forever. My father grumbles; my mother sighs.

One evening, as we sit around in the living room, my younger brother working on his homework, and my father reading the newspaper, my mother looks up from the banal magazine she has been leafing through to watch a program that has just commenced on television. It is the anniversary of the Islamic Revolution of February 1979, and the state channel is showing its version of the Pahlavi overthrow. Enormous crowds have gathered for the return to Tehran of the Ayatollah. And here is the Father of the Revolution himself, raising his hand to the ecstatic crowds. Now the program switches back to scenes of repression under the Shah. Brutish policemen chase protestors down the streets. Mullahs are humiliated by SAVAKI. Mothers gather at the gates of Evin Prison to plead for news of husbands and sons thought to be held inside. The unrelenting voice-over reminds viewers of the lawlessness of the Shah's henchmen. That's how it used to be, says the announcer. Thank God we no longer have to endure the indignity of living under the rule of a godless despot like Mohammad Reza Shah Pahlavi!

My mother shakes her head and clucks her tongue as she watches, growing more and more vexed. When she can stand it no more, she begins a long lament for the passing of the Pahlavis. She speaks of the life we used to live, of the happiness we once knew. How much more comfortable we'd been in those days! I listen, but I'm not convinced. My father, watching the celebrations, winces and shrugs and occasionally guffaws. But he says little.

Later that evening, when my mother comes to say goodnight to me in bed, I ask her about the old days. I know what she will say, of course, but I am interested in testing how far she will go. It's a little cold-blooded of me, I confess. My mother sits on the side of my bed and looks to the side, then fixes her gaze on the far-off in the way that people do when they recall the past.

She speaks of the picnics in the parks, the camping holidays, the abundance of food in the market. She tells me of the annual gatherings of senior military officers and their families in the grounds of the Imperial Palace in North Tehran, all invited by the Shah as an expression of his gratitude for their diligence and loyalty. Tables are set up in the sunshine under the cedars and spruce. There is exquisite food and lovely wine. The nation's best singers and musicians entertain this congregation of the elite. Acrobats perform breathtaking leaps and tumbles.

My mother, who adores social gatherings of this sort involving her whole family, chats happily with her women friends, and calls her children to her side proudly and shows them off, fending off compliments in the super-polite way of Persians while inwardly bursting with pleasure: 'You think Zarah is pretty? Oh, perhaps a little. But too thin, surely! Now, your Miriam, why she is a princess, as fair as any girl in Iran!' The band plays a medley of popular favourites, including Western hits. Such a day! And there stands her husband in his immaculate uniform, the single most handsome male between Kermanshah and Zahedan, from the Caspian coast to Bandar Abbas.

'Oh, Zarah! Oh darling! Such times! Do you know, Zarah, people were happy then. We were all so happy. We had a king, a good king. Everybody loved the Shah and his wife — such a beautiful woman, Farah. So gracious, so kind. People used to thank the Almighty for their lives. Such happiness, darling! Such happiness!'

I know this is only part of the truth. Some of us were happy, yes; but many, many were not. How could a revolution like Khomeini's succeed in a land of happy, contented people? Did millions upon millions of Iranians say, 'Oh, we're so pleased with our lives that we want to give up all sorts of freedoms and make our land a pariah amongst the nations of the world so that we can be happier still?' But I let Mum continue her reverie, biding my time and fashioning my put-down.

Sometimes I look away from the rapture of my mother's expression to gaze at the pictures on the walls of my bedroom – a bedroom that is all mine, now that my three older sisters are married. A photographic portrait of Kafka with dark, luminous eyes stares back at me from above my bookcase. To his right hangs a painted portrait of Hedayat, a wonderful Iranian novelist. Above these two portraits hangs a Zoroastrian icon, an angel in a circle of fire, one hand raised in benediction. Further to Kafka's left I have placed my treasured poster of Michael Jackson moon-walking, copied from the original brought back from America by a girlfriend. On the wall behind Mum hangs a set of shelves on which my travel souvenirs are displayed, for I am an irremediably soppy collector of knick-knacks from Iranian cities: a statuette of Darius the Great from Shiraz; ceramics from Esfahan; a little wooden ship from the Caspian coast. The ornaments and the Zoroastrian icon enjoy the wholehearted approval of my mother – and why not, since these are the very sort of things she has filled our entire apartment with. Hedayat she can tolerate, although his subject matter is a worry to her; Kafka is alarming; Michael Jackson makes her nervous.

Mum is still speaking of the glory of the past, delighted to be given the opportunity. Who else can she speak to in this way? My father is hardly likely to listen for more than a minute or two; it isn't his thing. If he wants to speak of the old days, it is usually to make a political point, comparing suffrage under the Shah with the mock-suffrage of the mullahs, who reserve a power of veto over anything the electorate might endorse (and so did the Shah, but his vetoes were 'more sensible', whatever that means ... but best not mention that). My sisters are prepared to listen to Mum's rhapsodies off-and-on; my brothers hardly at all. No, I am the best listener, although my listening this evening is utterly self-serving.

Mum pauses for breath and, with all the egotism, not to mention the cruelty, of my sixteen years, I say, 'Mum, you're dreaming. It just wasn't like that.'

'Yes, darling. It was. I swear.'

'Sure.'

'Every word, darling. It was just like that.'

I gaze at my mother's face, full of tender concern for me. What will become of a girl who doesn't wish to believe in such stories? I grimace, but I know it is unkind to persist. There is no shaking my mother's convictions about the land of happiness that once was; the land of milk and honey and annual parties in the palace grounds. But in my heart, I say no. Even as I reach out to take my mother's hand and place it on my cheek, I say no.

This is how my treachery began. This is how I became a traitor. It was not by deciding to record all the injustice and lies and hyprocrisy and greed in the Iran that I grew up in, and deciding to put them into a dossier labelled, 'The wicked land of the wicked mullahs', but by doubting what I was told. Once you doubt, there is hope. Once you distrust, there is hope. Of what use to anyone are pretty fantasies? And of what use are ugly fantasies? In all of my conversations with kids of my own age who were fed up, like me, with pompous men telling us what to do and think and wear and believe, I never came across one who believed that everything would be rosy if only the monarchy were restored. What, replace one tyranny with another? No.

chapter seventeen

I am lying on my stinky blanket in my cell, tortured by an idea so disturbing that it is making me tremble. This is the idea: I am here suffering not because of my splendid political beliefs, but because of my capacity for hero-worship.

I picture myself arriving at university on the first day of semester. I am frightened, but also delighted. Oh, the things I will learn! The people I will meet! How diligently I will study, how devotedly I will honour my teachers! And they will be so impressed with me — my teachers, my professors, my lecturers! 'Have you noticed that clever girl in languages? Zarah, I think her name is. Keep an eye on her; she's going places, that one.' I am too shy to approach anyone at first. I stand about in the square under the London Plane trees with my girlfriends and giggle. But if any of the professors pass by, I put on a deeply serious expression and gaze straight ahead, as if some powerful realisation about the nature of existence has gripped me.

I soon learn the rules of cool. Do I want the professors to think I'm some bumpkin from the dusty backlots of the country? I wear my scarf a little further back on my head, allowing more of my hair to show. My scarf itself is far from standard-issue: it's dark, yes, but it has a pattern of small blue-and-red dots. I make sure that, when I walk about in the square or along the corridors, I saunter; I try to show my sophistication in my very gait. Whenever I cross the path of the insufferable Basijis, I glance at them with pitying disdain, hoping that my insolence is being noticed by the university's elite.

Of all the people I hope to impress, Arash is foremost. The well-behaved students, those who have no argument whatsoever with the regime, always look at Arash as if he were liable to snatch them from the bosom of their families and carry them off to hell, leaving nothing behind but the echo of his demonic laugh. But to the would-be cool, like me, he is the Gary Cooper of the campus – the guy with that gentle something about him who nevertheless wears a six-shooter strapped to his waist and is ready to face the bad guys at High Noon. I don't really have to rely on Hollywood for a model of comparison: Arash is, in fact, a hero in the great tradition of Persian heroes. He is Rustam in his daring and bravery; he is Darius the Great in his regal disdain for the pettiness of lesser princes; he is Omar Khayyam in his satirical disregard of conventions and protocols; he is Hafiz in his romantic swagger.

I adore him.

I gather up all my nerve one day and approach him in the corridor. I stand nearby while he is chatting with other students older than me. An opportunity comes for me to say something that shows whose side I am on politically, and I squeak something out – nothing so arresting as, 'Death to the mullahs!' but something that is meant to convey my deep thoughtfulness and also my amazing wit. Arash looks at me with amusement; the older students look at me with mild contempt. Later in the week, I take myself off to a campus political meeting, and Arash is there. When he sees me scurry in and take a seat, he turns in his own seat and smiles at me over his shoulder. I push my scarf a little further back, put on my most fierce anti-regime expression, and Arash laughs out loud. Humiliation runs through me like a white fire; I feel as if I might almost burst into tears, but I keep my seat, somehow.

With persistence, I come to know Arash better, and he is a little more prepared to tolerate me. I tell him all about my contempt for the regime, and of the heights I have scaled in my advocacy of radical change. 'Big plans,' he says, still amused. 'You know, we don't expect to change very much. A few little things this time round, a few more next time. You sound like one of those kids who signed up for martyrdom in the war – those kids who couldn't wait to die for the cause. Slow down, little one.'

So I slow down. My anti-regime rhetoric becomes calmer. I tell my friends, old ones from high school and new ones from university, that 'we' (me and all the most senior people in the movement) only want to change a few little things this time round, and a few more next time. We are not firebrands, I say; we are not martyrs. Goodness knows what my friends made of this new pose; but whatever it was, they were kind enough not to tell me.

In spite of adopting this new posture of extreme cool, I still follow Arash about like a puppy dog, stopping where he stops, starting again when he starts. Anyone watching could see how besotted I am. My infatuation is romantic, it's true, but it's not that I expect to go to bed with Arash, and marry him and raise a big brood of radical children. Women (but certainly not men) are capable of loving to distraction without surrendering completely to the erotic. Or if the erotic complement is there, women can keep it under control, enjoying the sheer thrill of loving, with the kissing and embracing left in abeyance. Women cannot love like this forever – sooner or later we want to touch and be touched – but we can maintain it for quite a time.

Now I come to the part of my worship of Arash that distresses me: what if he had been an ugly little guy with great big teeth jutting out of his face who sprayed spittle when he talked? Were not his good looks and Byronic postures part of his attraction? And, spiritually, would I have been so besotted if he were indifferent to the suffering of others? Wasn't it his gentleness that formed such a part of his allure? Was it true, perhaps, that I saw in him the ideal dad, no more handsome than my dad (well, few men are, in all candour), but a dad I could fall for? See, this is the trouble with reading a bit of Freud – you begin to see ten possible motives where there was only one before.

Three days ago I was sick to death of Arash, and brimming with scorn for his birds and poems and his rallying calls. Now I am besotted again. What on earth am I? Just a reed that bends in the wind? Surely there is a core to me? And if there truly is a core to me, Arash should be there, surely? He has been arrested a number of times and so the interrogators will be merciless with him, yet he somehow found the strength to leave me a message of encouragement. If I can't find the strength for anything else at all, at least let me honour Arash's bravery.

I lie here whimpering, then the whimperings cease and something intense comes into my brain – a focus, a frame that fits around my feelings. I knew what I was doing. I knew I was getting into trouble. I knew it. It wasn't just Arash; he lent the aura to all that I was experiencing, but he wasn't the core that the aura surrounds. There is a Zarah at the heart of me. 'Because listen, listen! (I am talking aloud to myself now.) She knows they have made her weak and broken and pathetic, but that is just pain and fear. We all know that pain and fear work. We all know that torture works. What's the big news there? Okay, you tortured her; she would have said anything to make you stop. She could do the same to you, and so can anyone do the same to anyone else. But if she ever gets out of here, she will be scared, that's true, and maybe she won't run out into the streets and start shouting again. All the same, she doesn't believe a single word of what you want her to believe! She doesn't believe a single word of it, you liars!'

I am going mad, but it's lovely. I am as mad as my dear madman. I talk of myself in the third person. I make up little fantasies. Before long, I will be screaming out somebody's name, some fantasy lover's name who betrayed me, my Leila.

I stand and put my mouth close to the fan grille.

'Sohrab? Listen, do you want to talk about Leila?'

My madman doesn't answer. Maybe he's in one of his moods. This is such a pity, because now we have an even greater kinship. We are both mad. I'm annoyed that he won't answer me. I have the feeling that I could say extraordinary things at the moment. My brain is perfectly clear and mad at the same time. Surely that is what happens when you are mad. You believe that you alone can see things clearly, and that those around you live in a fog.

Oh, but that lovely mad clarity of thought is fading even as I stand here waiting for Sohrab to reply to me. I am becoming miserable and wretched again. It was only a holiday, the lovely madness.

I sit again on my stinky blanket and wipe the tears from my eyes. I am weak again. I am prepared to plead with the guards, with the interrogator. 'Be nice to me. I am no threat. I'm weak and disgusting, like a worm. If you want me to wriggle across the floor like a worm, of course I will do it. Tell me what you want me to do. No matter how awful, I will do it.'

The great thinkers, the great philosophers, want us to believe that suffering is ennobling: it makes you a finer person; it builds character. Well, I have to tell the great thinkers something else that is true: suffering corrupts you. It's okay if you already have character and wisdom and courage; but if you don't, suffering won't build such things in your heart and soul. It will consume what little courage you have, and then you are left with nothing. You see the man with the axe and the hood on his head. The wooden block sits before you. 'Bend your neck,' the axeman says through his hood in a muffled voice. 'Bend your neck.' Nothing can save you, so you might as well die with dignity. Except that there is no dignity left in you. Where your dignity was, there is only fear screeching for rescue, like rats in a cage screeching for release. Suffering has not made you strong. You look up at the axeman; you see the glint of the blade. 'Bend your neck,' he says. But, instead, you beg him to spare you, to forgive you. 'Not me!' you plead. 'Not me. Please, not me!'

chapter eighteen

We are what would be termed 'liberals' in my family, all of us: my father and mother, my older brothers, my sisters, even my younger brother. So are my cousins and nieces and nephews, and my uncles and aunts. We don't like dogma, we don't trust ideology, we want everyone to be free. We are pretty comfortable with the idea of boys and girls kissing and cuddling before marriage, and we don't mind much if the kissing and cuddling doesn't even lead to marriage. And everyone can wear what they like. If you wish to go shopping on Revolution Boulevard in a bikini, do so. It might not seem to us in the best possible taste, but go ahead, hussy. Everyone can read what they like. We are against censorship, mostly.

We are also in favour of a separation of church and state. Let the priests and mullahs make the law within their mosques and cathedrals, and let those who enter there obey the laws of the mosques and cathedrals. Once outside, let the Muslims and Christians and Jews observe the laws of a secular state. We are for capitalism, yes, but with an acceptable face, or at least a reasonably attractive mask; welfare, yes; tolerance, yes. We don't stand out from most middle-class Iranians in our politics; most are like us, though they are cautious about expressing their politics, just as we are – or as some of us are.

But then there is Ellie, my cousin, fourteen years old, going on forty.

Ellie is a true Child of the Revolution. Like me, she has lived her entire life under the rule of the mullahs. But in Ellie's case the message of the mullahs got through.

'Zarah,' she warned me when I was dating Behnam, 'take care not to have sex with your boyfriend before you are married. You will go to hell.'

'Zarah,' she censured me when she saw me indoors without my burka, dressed in jeans and a top that showed my middle, 'God can see inside.'

Being lectured to by a fourteen-year-old can be charming, if maddening at the same time, but Ellie had no intention of charming anyone. Her business was to save souls, and she had no doubt as to how to go about it because her teachers at school, her teachers on the radio and on television, her teachers at the mosque, had all provided her with a simple program of salvation: when you see the Law of God ignored, speak up. Ellie's zealousness became so feared within our extended family that we made efforts to comply with her rules whenever she was around. We weren't concerned that she would report us to the Basijis, or anything like that; she loved us, and it would never have occurred to her to land us in trouble. No, we were simply afraid of her frowns and her tut-tutting, and so we pandered to her in the way that people indulge a censorial grandparent. Her own parents did the same. I drew the line at wearing my headscarf indoors, but I kept as much of the rest of me covered up as I could to placate her. I didn't utter any criticisms of the regime when she was within earshot. If someone important to her was talking on the television – some revered Ayatollah, some grey-whiskered bigot – I excused my conscience from contributing a volley of abuse.

Sometimes I would study her in horrified fascination as she sat quietly, piously reading through tracts from the Koran, her expression one of clear and perfect faith. I watched her at other times as she assisted my mother in the kitchen: she, a girl in her teens; and my mother, a matron of fifty, and nothing to distinguish the two of them so far as conscientious attention to the needs of the household was concerned. Ellie was ready, while still a kid, to step straight into the role of obedient housewife and strict-but-affectionate mother. She had taught herself to work rapidly in the kitchen with one hand, using the other to keep her scarf drawn tight under her chin. This is a skill known to the wives of the more pious of the regime's supporters. For women like my mother, letting your head scarf hang loose while you work with both hands is perfectly acceptable.

In our household, as I was growing up, so many opinions were held in common that we were able to rely on a shorthand of gesture and expression to take the place of outbursts. We would see on the news that some poor young girl had been sentenced to death for having an affair and we would shake our heads, or put a hand over our eyes, or simply sigh deeply and mutter something like, 'Dreadful!' We lived in a circle of shared sympathies. Although I was well used to Ellie's tut-tutting and tsk-tsking and fussing, I suppose I must have believed that, deep down, she was still one of us. She might have tedious views on sin and redemption, but she would never endorse the more brutal ways of the regime.

Except that she did. Practices that were as merciless (and made about as much sense) as medieval trial-by-ordeal appeared perfectly just to Ellie. She accepted, for instance, the legal requirement for a male family member to confirm any charge of rape that a woman might make — just utter nonsense. And yet she was not heartless; not at all. She was a gentle girl who fretted over birds with damaged wings and stray doggies getting by on what they could find in rubbish bins and gutters. In many ways, even most ways, she was a marshmallow. She would come to my bedroom and sit on my bed, stroking my hand and touching my hair and talking endless, affectionate nonsense. But if I were cruel enough to experiment in the way I did with my mother when asking her to recall the glories of the Shah's regime, and ask Ellie about specific infamies perpetrated by her beloved mullahs, she would caution me in a kindly, grandmotherly way. 'Please believe me, teachers know many things that ordinary people don't know. They tell us what is best, Zarah.'

Raising concrete issues closer to home distressed Ellie, without seriously shaking her faith in the mullahs. Her aunt, divorced from an intolerable bully of a husband, asked Ellie in my hearing if she was happy with the way 'your people' made it impossible for her to see her own children — for that is the law in Iran. You can get a divorce if you're a woman, but you have to say goodbye to the kids. Ellie had seen my poor aunt in terrible states of distress over the children, yearning for the touch of a hand. And, watching in my rather clinical way, I thought, *A-ha! Wriggle out of this one, little darling!* Well, Ellie did wriggle; I could see the conflict in her eyes. There stood her aunt, dark circles under her eyes, half-insane with grief; never would there be a better reason for Ellie to murmur some reservations. But what she finally said was what might have been predicted – a version of the caution she had given me: 'About such things, I cannot know until I am grown. But my teachers will tell me. I will ask.'

The teachers, the teachers!

Is that all it comes down to – your choice of teachers? My teachers made the world of difference to my life, and I suppose the same could be said of Ellie's. But pray to God there's a little more to it than that, because who could fail to notice that the most zealous teachers are attracted to dogma? Give me a teacher, please, who is sometimes beset by doubt, who might answer your question by saying, 'I'll have to go away and think about that.' Take my beloved Omar Khayyam. He spent a great part of his life searching for certainty, only to conclude that the search is not only futile, but distracts you from the vigour of the life around you.

Dear Omar, under your bough with your jug of red wine of Shirazi grapes, your loaf of bread, and your girl. May the people of my country who live by the certainties of the mullahs come as one to their senses, pack a picnic lunch, and head for the parks and forests with their wives, their girlfriends, their husbands, and their boyfriends. May they kiss and gambol into the evening. May their children fall asleep under the stars and awake wondering what joys the day will bring. May Ellie awake with her chador fallen to her shoulders, and may she smile at the touch of the sun on her hair.

Oh, dream on, Zarah! But it's a lovely dream.

chapter nineteen

I have put out the green slip of paper to show the guard that I need to go to the toilet, but he isn't paying any attention. Sometimes I put the green slip out just to vary my day, but not this time. I pace up and down my cell – three short steps one way, three steps back – clutching my bladder. This will be the fourth time tonight I've needed to pee. Is there something wrong with my kidneys? Have I become ill in here? Surely the guards can extend a little lenience. It's not as though I am likely to make a run for it on the way to the toilet, overpower the armed guards, and steal the keys to a half-dozen doors. I just want to pee!

I begin to moan as I pace, aching for relief. If the guard doesn't come soon, I'll have to go on the floor of the cell. Maybe that's what they want me to do, so that they can scoff. Why should they bother? Is humiliating me more such a great achievement? Don't they know how easy it is to reduce a human being to the level of an animal? It doesn't require skill or magnificent insight. Dignity is the first thing you give up, when you have to. Not all at once, but bit by bit. Dignity becomes a luxury that you can no longer afford, like perfumes and scented soap and lipsticks from Paris. You can get by without it.

'Please!' I whimper, not so much for the guard as for God. 'Please, please!' Sweat is breaking out on my face from the effort of keeping control. Please let me keep this last thing, the feeling that I can keep my cell clean, just this last thing! But even that need is rapidly losing its force. Would it matter if the floor of my cell was wet? How could the cell smell worse than it does, in any case? I can feel the urge to surrender gaining control over me, but at the same time I know that when I am sitting here with a pool of my own urine around me, I will have lost something I wanted to keep. It's not even dignity. I think it must be to do with the idea of place that belongs to me. The cell belongs to me.

Even when they finish with me after an interrogation, I come back to this tiny place and it's mine. When the door slams shut, what is left of me is protected by these concrete walls. It's horrible to have to admit it, but this place is my home and I want it to be a clean home. It must be the homemaker in me. If I had the opportunity, I would put a little vase of flowers in the corner and a mat at the door. I would sweep the floor each day, maybe twice a day, and once a week I would get down on my hands and knees with a bucket of hot water and suds and scrub the concrete. I would put up a poster, maybe my Kafka poster from my bedroom in the home I used to have. Or maybe not Kafka. I love to gaze at the picture of Kafka when I am safe, but here it wouldn't be right. This place is a little too much like the places he wrote about. But please just let my cell be clean!

This is the truth about me. I am a simple, middle-class girl full of middle-class silliness. I want a husband and babies and a nice kitchen with a food-processor and a pop-up toaster and a vertical grill and one of those special kettles designed by some genius all made of stainless steel and looking like it belongs in an art gallery. I want a proper oven for the kitchen — very big, much bigger than I really need, white on the outside and with lots of little red lights that tell you what it's doing and how long things have been cooking. Also a big set of beautiful plates and bowls, and those small bowls that are made especially for deserts; and glasses, too, crystal glasses for wine; and a set of saucepans all the same, only some bigger than others. It's crazy for me to have such a desire for a beautiful kitchen because I can't cook, and I know nothing about shopping for a family or even for myself. Yet the beautiful kitchen sits there in my dream home, waiting for the day when I have learned to cook and have learned to choose a man who will make a lovely husband, instead of some business type with his head full of deals – Behnam, I'm thinking of, who could have made me very happy if he'd tried just a little harder.

I am gritting my teeth now with the effort of not peeing. I bend over and tighten my arms around my middle. I think I might be able to last another ten seconds, and then I will go on the floor and to hell with my home!

Ten seconds pass, and many more, hundreds more, before the guard comes to my cell. I want to kill him. I want to push my fingernails into the flesh of his face and leave deep, bleeding wounds. As soon as he opens the door, I have to clamp my mouth shut on the words that spring onto the tip of my tongue – horrible swear words, foul words that I never normally use. I can't insult him. He can easily push me back into the cell and slam the door shut on me again.

'How many times do you go to the toilet in a day?' he says. 'This is the fourth time. No more.'

'I'm sorry,' I say meekly. 'I'm not feeling well.'

'Well, too bad about that. We didn't invite you to come here. You invited yourself.'

As soon as I close the toilet door behind me and relieve my aching bladder, I glimpse a message on the back of the door. It's from Arash. I don't even try to read it. I just enjoy the happiness of peeing. Finally, I look back at the message and read it. It says, 'Be strong. B is trying for you.' The 'B' stands for 'Behnam', as I realise immediately; but then, for a few seconds, I have no further comprehension of the message. Then my eyes are flooded with tears; not just a trickle, but a downpour, a monsoon. My face is so sodden that I can feel the drops merging into small streams and running off my chin. Oh, I have never cried like this!

I replace the blindfold, and step out of the cubicle and into the hands of the guard. He can see the tears running out from under the blindfold. Unexpectedly, he touches my shoulder, very lightly. 'I will take you to the toilet again tonight,' he says quietly. 'If you need to go, I will take you.'

'Thank you. Thank you.'

I stop the tears while I am being escorted back to my cell. But once the door is closed and I have put the blindfold back out through the slot, I let this great storm of emotion have its way with me. I don't even know where all this stuff is coming from! So Behnam is trying for me? Good for him! If he'd tried for me a little earlier, I wouldn't have so much to weep about. The tears gush down my face, as if some great organ of my body, something bigger than my heart or even my liver, is pumping up huge volumes of water and channelling it all to my eyes.

When the tears finally abate, I am left sitting on my stinky blanket with a hairless head and a face that must look like that of a scarecrow out in the rain. If Behnam could see me now, he might think again about doing something for me, about getting me out of this hellish place. Does he still think of me as his girlfriend? Poor man, such a girlfriend! These people in Evin have beaten all of the girlfriend out of me. I wouldn't wish my ugly self on any man in Iran.

But what exactly can Behnam do? I try to work it out sensibly. Can I really begin to believe that there is a way out of here for me? Is that possible? Behnam knows a lot of powerful people – he has connections galore – but I'm reluctant to plant the seed of hope in my heart, for I know that Behnam will always think of his reputation first if he has to choose between altruism and assisting an enemy of the regime. He won't want to jeopardise his business arrangements with these foul people who run my country. And then there is his mum. She has always considered me unsuitable for her son. I'm too much of a hothead for her darling boy, and I'm no good at cooking, can't mend anything with a needle and thread, have no interest at all in learning all that stuff you're supposed to know about keeping your man happy and content. She doesn't know about my dream house with the dream kitchen, and she doesn't know how much I want to look down at the face of my own baby and see his tiny hands reaching up towards my face. She just sees a snooty girl spouting quotations from books she doesn't like the sound of. Well, too bad about me. If she thinks her son can do better, let him go and search.

Anyway, why is Arash leaving me messages about Behnam when he doesn't even like Behnam? Each of them used to scoff when I mentioned the other's name. Behnam used to call Arash a 'peasant' – I think because Arash came from outside Tehran, and super-sophisticated Tehranis pretend to believe that all of Iran outside Tehran is a wilderness populated by cavemen. One time, the two of them even came to the brink of punching each other. I can't even remember what it was about. Probably Arash was talking about the corruption and deceit of the regime, and Behnam probably said something sarcastic. The odd thing is,

Behnam actually respects Arash, in his way. He knows that Arash is far braver than he. He knows that he would never risk what Arash risks each day.

Oh, but if Behnam still wants me, why should I pretend that it's all a matter of indifference to me? For the love of God, if he wants me, he can have me. I'll marry him. If he gets me out of here, I'll have his babies one after the other, and I'll wear chador, and underneath I'll wear Louis Vuitton stuff and frilly underwear, just like the wives of his friends do. I'll go to his idiotic parties, and stay with the wives, and tell them how ecstatic I am that my children have learned to recite passages from the Koran, and go into fresh gales of praise when I tell the wives how Behnam follows Mohammad with such devotion. I will do anything for Behnam, anything on earth — never even once mention politics again in my whole remaining life, if only he gets me out of here. I don't care the tiniest bit about detesting myself. Let me detest myself until I burst, I don't care!

—

Another day with no interrogation. I don't want an interrogation, so why am I restless? I should be overjoyed. It's just that every part of me is tired of waiting for whatever is to happen to me. Each part is tired in its own way. My legs and arms feel as if they are made of soft spaghetti; there are no bones in them, no blood. My feet are not only tired but are growing soft on the soles through lack of exercise. Pacing up and down my little cell isn't going to provide them with what they need. The skin of my face feels like that of an aged grandmother that you see on the streets, pale and creased.

I sit and look around my cell, switching my gaze from one wall to another, then to the door, then to the floor. My eyes are famished. They yearn for something to feast on. I wish a bug would visit me – an ant, a mosquito, a fly, a cockroach, any sort of bug at all, just so long as I could use my vision and notice things about the bug that my brain would then go to work on. It's strange, but when you sit around with no stimulation for your sight or your brain, and nothing for your muscles to do, your body blames you, as if it were you who had chosen to impose this fast of the senses and the muscles. So when I get to my feet and pace these three short steps one way and three short steps back, it is because some angry and impatient being inside me is saying, 'You! Do something! Walk! Read a book! Go to a movie! What's the matter with you?'

No friendly bug comes to stir my senses, and so I reluctantly allow my brain to indulge in its one recreation: imagining murder. This comes over me each day, and I always resist it for a time and always give in, like someone who knows it is a sin to find erotic gratification all alone, and promises to stop, and can't stop, and promises again, and again breaks the promise. It is always the fat man who is my victim. Sometimes he walks into my cell alone, gloating and snorting, thinking that I am completely at his mercy; but what he doesn't know is that I have found some way to arm myself with a big hammer, such as those I have seen labourers using when they are replacing cobblestones on the street. Yes, it is a very big hammer that I have concealed behind my back; and, as I watch the fat man approach (for I have refused to wear my blindfold), I am conscious of the great weight of my weapon, so aware of its deadliness. But do I give the slightest hint of the weapon I am holding with both my hands, out of sight of this pig? No, none at all. I wear an expression of girlish fear that delights him all the more. I simulate a trembling all over my body. I seem to be saying, 'Oh dear, what can I do, what can I do? My situation is — well, it's just hopeless! Oh dear, oh dear!' Then, when he is close enough for his vile breath to sicken me, the gloating in his face at its most repulsive, I bring the hammer out from behind me and smash it down on his melon skull with all my strength. For a moment he appears undamaged, merely staring back at me with a puzzled expression. But wait, wait! Because now, see! See how his head breaks in half and the hideous mess within erupts from the gape, and pours down his chest and his piggy gut!

Oh, it's more wonderful than anything! More, more, more wonderful!

But sick.

Within a minute of the fantasy's completion, I am full of disgust with myself, ill with self-loathing.

No more of that, Zarah! No more!

—

I've just had a shower, my third in what I think is the three weeks I've been here. The water on my scalp made me shriek, for I've been scratching at my stubble, scratching uncontrollably, and it's all a bloody mess up there.

And I need to shave my legs. I hate going about with hairy legs. It makes me fret and grizzle. It occurs to me that they — the people who run this foul place — probably know how long it takes for a girl like me to deteriorate physically and fall to bits. Maybe they have a chart on a wall somewhere, and they tick off items as they notice them: losing weight; becoming haggard; skin gone dry and itchy; shaved scalp scratched and bleeding; muscles turning to jelly; soles of the feet softening; menstrual cycle interrupted; legs getting hairy. And what's next? Do my teeth fall out?

I sit with my face buried in my hands, wondering if I'll ever be pretty again. I was used to being pretty. It was so nice! I know how shallow it is to be wishing to have my prettiness back, but it was mine and it was lovely, and I was never vain; I never went about preening myself and feeling gorgeous. Well, in fact I did now and again, but I just thought of it as good fortune, I didn't think it made me a better person.

Where is Sohrab? Why isn't he making any sounds up there? Have they taken him away to interrogate him? What could they possibly hope to learn from someone who has been here for ten years or more? He doesn't know anything about the world outside. Surely they don't take him to a cell and torture him just for the pleasure of it!

Oh, where is my madman?

I close my eyes and whisper a prayer for Sohrab. I ask God to spare him more beatings, more torture. I ask God to give my poor madman back.

Prayers, prayers, prayers! Is there some enormous archive somewhere in heaven or hell where all the prayers of those who begged and pleaded are kept? Those who prayed and pleaded without hope? Forgotten prayers in folders, gathering dust?

I rock my head side-to-side with my face in my hands, with my hands resting against my raised knees.

chapter twenty

I f you were born in Kermanshah province in the west of Iran, you are still an Iranian but, in all likelihood, an Iranian of a different sort. Kermanshah and its two neighbouring provinces of Kordestan and Zanjan are home to most of Iran's five million Kurds. Having most of Iran's Kurds cooped up in the west suits all of the non-Kurdish Iranians just fine, for Kurds are considered weird in some ways and nuisances in other ways. My mother and father are both Kurdish, both born in Kermanshah, and so I am a Kurd. I'm happy to be thought of as weird in some ways and a nuisance in other ways.

The Kurds are the oldest ethnic group in Iran's part of the Middle East. They've been there for 4000 years, and their roots go down to soils created by gods who lived in fire and ruled by magic. Such places still exist in the world; places where visitors, all unaware, suddenly sense something strange, as if the air above these ancient soils is full of fugitive whispers. That magic of the gods of fire still feeds into the blood of Kurds; and even though they are mostly Muslim, other Muslims consider Kurdish Islamism primitive and full of pagan impurities. And on top of the pagan impurities, Kurds are Sunnis, which makes them even more suspect to the majority Shi'ites of Iran — in something of the way that a Protestant minority in a country might be regarded with suspicion by a large Catholic majority.

It was the Kurds who gave me the heart and soul I have had to rely on all these years; and in particular it was my grandma, my father's mother, who taught me the Kurdish language and plaited into my consciousness the ancient beliefs and customs of these strange people. I must concede that many of these customs and beliefs were ritualised superstitions (secretly putting salt in the shoes of a visitor to your house whose return was undesired; telling fortunes by running fingers through the subject's hair; sleeping while pregnant with a holy book under your pillow; keeping wedding celebrations running for precisely seven days, seven being a sacred number), but it all went to my heart.

I spent my early years seeking the company of my grandma, both in Tehran, where she lived part of the year with my family, and on visits to Kermanshah, the great city of Kermanshah province, when Grandma was staying with my uncle's family. I was the only one of her grandchildren who found the sort of delight in her stories and language that she was hoping to pass on, and I think this was because of a knack for languages that must have been nestled in my genes when I was born, waiting to have its say in my life.

What sparked this knack was my realisation that the same message could be conveyed in the different words of a different language. I can't claim to recall the moment when this dawned on me, but I know there must have been a day and an hour when I fashioned something from my grandma's language, and so grasped this amazing fact. A pomegranate in Farsi was still a pomegranate in Kurdish, only its name came out of my mouth specially altered for Grandma.

Grandma was a widow in all the years I knew her. Her husband had died when she was still quite young, and her children had been taken from her to live with her brother-in-law's family. Such is the law in Iran, and a truly wicked law it is. My poor grandma had to walk a round-trip of six hours to see her children – something she did regularly and without a murmur of complaint, as if it were a labour of love. I think, in some ways, the closeness that grew up between my grandma and me expressed years of Grandma's underemployed affection for her own children, and gave her the opportunity to fuss and adore and cosset and teach a child in the way that had been denied her.

I was a glutton for affection and pampering as a child, as if my mother's endless endearments merely whetted my appetite for more and more. I went everywhere with Grandma – to the market, to the bazaar, to the homely little shops of her Kurdish friends. I came to think of the way my grandma dressed as a model for myself when I grew older; her beautiful long hair exposed in the Kurdish manner, wrapped only at the back in a coiled scarf or a headband; her long, colourful dresses. We resembled each other in a way that went beyond the physical: I gestured in the way she did, tilted my head in just the same manner to express wonderment, smiled in the same way. No doubt I learned these things from Grandma, but perhaps there is room to speculate on the inheritance of a matching set of genes, too.

Kurds have been, for a long, long time, an unlucky people, never free to draw a border and say, 'This is our land, the nation of the Kurds.' They live like impoverished second cousins on the fields of more fortunate relatives; at best, they are pitied or ridiculed; at worst, hunted and killed by their relatives for not showing enough gratitude. They spill over into Turkey, Iraq,

MY LIFE AS A TRAITOR

Syria; and wherever they are found, they are a minority. Those who rule them regard them as a burden. I know from what I have read that the Kurds have always wanted a homeland, but have never had the luck or maybe the skill to win great, decisive battles to secure one. Fierceness in fighting has never been a handicap; bravery has never been a problem. Like most of the peoples of the Middle East, Kurds will rise at dawn on the first day of the week, if need be, and fight without thought of rest or sustenance for the next seven days. The great leader, the military genius, the merciless egomaniac who spreads his influence far and wide – no, the Kurds have never produced such a man, and so they keep to their mountains and by turns accept their oppressors' rule, and rebel against it.

I can't speak with any intimate knowledge of the Kurds of Turkey and Iraq, but I do know that thousands of years of being ruled by others has bred a type of versatility into the Kurds of Iran – or into some, at least. These versatile Kurds are the ones who are not driven by a passion for a homeland of their own, but for equality within the borders of Iran. My father is a Kurd of this sort. He employed his military and administrative talents in the service of the Shah; then, when the Shah was deposed, he turned his hand to business and found a way of getting along with the mullahs. His priority always was the survival of his family; not on any terms, but on terms of equality.

My father has always been a pragmatist, except when it came to the question of leaving Iran altogether when the mullahs took charge in 1979. He had the opportunity to sell up and flee, but he stayed out of sheer love of country, and so ceded everything he owned to the regime. His versatility shows in the way in which he was able to accept that the Shah's reign was over, and to then cast about for some means to support his family. My father wants things to work in the best way they can, not in the best way that can be imagined. He is not an idealist; he is not altruistic. He draws lines in the sand indicating points from which he will not retreat, but he makes sure that the lines he draws provide latitude for movement. And this choice of pragmatism over passion is, I think, typical of the type of Kurd he is.

I am a Kurd of my father's sort; a versatile Kurd. I have no interest in the ultimate. I want things to work as well as they can, given human limitations. When I run into the street and shout and shake my fist, I am not shouting, 'Utopia or death!' I am shouting something much humbler: 'I want my pink shoes!' That would be enough, for once the mullahs have conceded my right to wear pink shoes, so much that is good and wise and kind and just plain *human* follows. I have no argument with Islam, not even with the career and progeny of the Prophet's nephew Ali or with forms of words in the Koran; my argument is with the mullahs.

It is the same argument I would have if I were Jewish and were compelled to live a life regulated by an unyielding Orthodox regime of Jewish mullahs; or if I were Catholic and had to listen to a Catholic mullah telling me that my flesh existed only to be mortified; or if I had to listen to a Buddhist mullah insisting that the joy and excitement of my lover's kiss is an illusion. Mullahs all over the world fear what women make them feel — that's my complaint. They seem to detest so much of what nature has provided. I am quite sure that human beings can contemplate the divine without denying their desires. I can do this, as can my girlfriends, and there's nothing special about us.

My father, as I say, is one of these versatile Kurds that I speak of, but it is my Kurdish mother who understands most about making the best of what is provided.

Western women think that the typical Iranian woman lives the life of a vassal, and I can understand why they think in this way. I know of many Iranian women — unmarried and married — whose lives are made miserable by the laws that regulate their days and nights. And nothing on earth can be said in defence of laws that permit the males of a society to hold the spirit of women hostage. Such laws are evil, wherever they are enacted. But the life of an Iranian woman, under a saner interpretation of the Koran than applies in Iran now, has much more in common with the lives of women in the West, or with women anywhere, than might be supposed. My mother lives under laws that Western women would probably think insufferable, but she is as free in her heart and soul as anyone on earth, male or female.

My mother's path to freedom grew out of her convictions, just as mine did; only my path ended in a swamp. For her, as for many women, freedom is love. I don't mean to say she lives in a pink mist and dreams of endless kisses in rose bowers; her vision of love is as tender as that, yes, but it is tougher, too. Love, for my mother, is something expressed with the hands even more than the heart. People may talk of their love, and talk and talk; but until they use their hands, the talk is only talk. My mother's hands are no longer as beautiful as they once were. When she strokes my cheeks and frames my face with her palms, and holds me captive so that I have no choice but to look her in the eyes, I can feel the roughness of her flesh. I could say that her hands show the wear and tear of being a woman, but I'd prefer to say that she has the hands that you earn after years and years of being a human being; years and years of hands-on interventions in the lives of your children, of your husband; years and years of approaching salvation in the humblest of ways.

These interventions of my mother's were not restricted to her family. Because of her knack for finding workable compromises, she was sought out by neighbours to find a path to peace. In Tehran, our neighbour had two wives, and had fathered five children with each. The combined ten children were more than those two wives could manage. Things would have been easier if the two wives had been able to get along with each other, but instead they were terrible rivals under the one roof. Their bitter arguments were known all over the neighbourhood, and people would shake their heads and cluck their tongues. Polygamy is frowned upon by middle-class Muslims; it is considered a relic of the past. Sharia law – the scriptural law that permits multiple marriage and a wide range of dreadful sanctions for crimes of certain sorts – is thought of in the same way: as cruel and degrading. But when my mother was called on by the two wives of our neighbour to make peace, she set aside her feelings about Sharia law and did what she always did: she looked for a way in which some dignity could be re-established. This was her policy.

As I've mentioned, whenever there was an argument within our family, my mother would descend like a ministering angel, forcing my brother to kiss me and apologise after he'd perpetrated some vile trick on me, and she would force him to call me 'Dear sister'. Of course, she couldn't compel the two wives of our neighbour to kiss and make up, but she would sit for hours listening to their bitter grievances, offering suggestions, soothing the agitated hands of each wife with her own hands.

Recalling my mother's addiction to peace-making makes me wish to lampoon her, and I'm certainly capable of that. But at a deeper level I see something that should be spared my sense of humour, something that has persisted in women for so many ages – and that is a deep distrust of abstractions. It is always much more difficult for a woman than for a man to say something like, 'All property should be shared, and those who don't wish to share must be put to death.' Or, 'It is God's will that those who dispute God's will should be thrown into the flames.' Or even, 'The world does not exist, and those who think it does exist must be disabused.' Women hold children in their hands; they wipe the snot from children's noses; they sit at bedsides soothing the child who has woken from a nightmare.

Men care for their children, too, very lovingly, and I would not wish to denigrate the contribution of the male parent in child-rearing. Nor would I say that women cannot in their nature be savage and ruthless. At the same time, it would surely be true to say that women historically have been in the better position to judge how much painstaking attention is required in rearing a child, and I think it could also be argued that they are less inclined than men of a certain sort to thrust their children into harm's way.

Women like my mother know that abstractions are useless in the day-to-day struggle to preserve the lives of children, and just as useless as a foundation for happiness. Of course, nothing much can be done about injustice if peaceful acceptance of the status quo is forever breaking out. But for women like my mother – versatile, practical, hands-on women – the injustices employed to overcome injustice can be foreseen, and any eventual victory will seem pyrrhic. My mother knows injustice when she sees it; it is only the path to justice that rouses her doubts and trepidation.

—

Amongst our neighbour's ten children there was one little girl named Azam. She had no self-confidence at all, and struggled to make herself heard in her rowdy family. She couldn't control her speech, and stuttered and blundered over simple statements. She was ridiculed within her family and without; ridiculed even by her father, our neighbour Ahmad Agha. At the time I knew Azam, Iraqi missiles were exploding in Tehran. All of the children in the targetted parts of Tehran, including my neighbourhood, saw things that should never make their way into children's heads: hills of rubble from which smoke rose in clouds, the material beneath the stone and concrete burning with a crackling sound; hands and arms and legs protruding from the burning debris — hands that still wore wedding rings, feet with the shoes blown away, and with toes that twitched; people staggering like zombies in the clear places between the hills of rubble, their clothing shredded on their bodies.

After the first missile bombardments, it felt to me as if some terrible mistake had been made, and that things I had heard of on the news and from my teachers about the deaths of martyrs on battlefields had broken out in the wrong place, by accident. It didn't seem possible to me that the fires and the screaming and the bleeding could have been made to happen on purpose, here where I lived. What I saw, Azam saw, and she ceased to talk at all — ceased trying to make her awkward and hesitating attempts at speech, at least — to anyone except me. I was her friend and supporter, through the intervention of my mother.

Her spiritual beliefs and, even more, her temperament, made it impossible for my mother to utter commands. Zoroastrianism is not a religion of instruction; and, in any case, Mum would have chosen to walk barefoot across Iran on broken glass if that were the one alternative to delivering a lecture. It was her strategy to act, then to nudge me very gently until my gaze fell on what she wanted me to see. When she took me shopping for a new dress (at the ages of five and six, it was okay for me to wear a dress, rather than a chador, in public), she would buy a second dress for Azam, who was exactly my age and exactly my size. 'And this one will be for Azam, of course,' she would say. If Azam was staying for lunch or dinner, Mum didn't badger her for answers to questions. 'Azam, you eat beet, I'm sure, but leave it on the plate if you don't.' If she did need the answer to a question, she would relay the question through me, sparing Azam the ordeal of speaking. And so, without even knowing it, I was adopting my mother's way of approaching Azam.

It's only now, as I write, that I understand the terrible distress I must have caused my mother when I went into the street to shake my fist at injustice. Acting in such a way would have contradicted every impulse that she had. It was dangerous, it was ill-mannered, it was immodest, it was irreligious. The gentle advice she had been offering me all her life without ever making a bold statement about it was that injustice has to be countered in a subtle, almost stealthy way. As I grew older and better understood how Azam's father abused her, I wanted to go next door and tell Arman Agha to go to hell, where he belonged. My mother wouldn't permit it. And when I spoke of the injustice of the mullahs, Mum would look at me in that embarrassed way parents have when they notice in the child they love with all their hearts something that in another person they would abhor.

My political activism, to my mother, was a form of vanity: a boast to the world of my moral beauty. This may not be true, but it's certainly true that if my mother could make everything work in the way she wanted, and I could make it all work in the way I wanted, most people would choose to live under my mother's regime.

chapter twenty-one

'Do you know what you sound like?' says Sohrab. 'You sound like an old widow, grumbling and grizzling about everything.'

It's true that I've been complaining – or grumbling and grizzling, if that's the way my madman wants to think of it. Complaining about my bleeding scalp, and my dry skin, and my muscles that have no strength in them. Oh, but I'm so relieved that he's back! He doesn't say where he has been and what has been done to him, and I don't ask. I'm frightened of what I might hear.

'Well, who wouldn't grizzle here?' I grizzle. 'I found myself chewing my nails, just before.'

'Why not? It keeps you busy.'

'Be serious!'

'I am being serious. Why not chew your nails? But don't do the other things. Don't hurt yourself. Some of them do that.'

'Do what?'

'Hurt themselves with their hands. Or hit their head on the wall to see their own blood. And don't chew all your nails in one day. Save some for other days so you'll have something to do.'

'You're not funny.'

'Do you think I'm joking with you? No. And you don't have to tell me what you look like. I know what you look like. Your skin is ugly; all of you is ugly. No oxygen, no vegetables, no moisturiser, no water. Not even proper sleep. You look like one of those girls you see on the streets in the night – girls who never eat properly and sleep in doorways.'

I should be offended by what Sohrab is saying about me, even though it's true. But I can't be offended. I'm too glad to have his voice back again to risk telling him to shut up. In any case, I have stopped worrying about not being pretty anymore. I don't care. I will never be pretty again. That's all gone.'

'And what about you?' I ask. 'Are you as handsome as ever?'

'Oh, more than before I came here. More. Bad food makes me beautiful.'

'I have to go to the toilet,' I tell Sohrab. 'Will you talk to me again when I get back?'

'Maybe.'

'Say yes or no!'

'Do you think that you can make me do what you want by being bossy?'

'I want you to talk to me when I get back from the toilet. Please.'

'Maybe,' he says.

All the way to the toilet, I think only about Sohrab. It's as if we are married. We're moody with each other, just like husbands and wives are. We argue for the sake of arguing, and that's what husbands and wives do. We want to know what the other one is doing all of the time. We resent each other for having a life apart from the relationship. If Sohrab were talking to another girl, perhaps in the cell above him, I would be mad with jealousy.

Talking to me is like being faithful to me. And then there are other things that husbands and wives enjoy, some of the time, at least: goodwill, affection. Or, in truth, it is more than affection with me. I feel that I love him. I can't bear to think of him being beaten by the guards. The idea of something worse than beating – torture – makes me wild, as if I could kill the people who would harm him with my hands and with whatever I could pick up. He is my madman. If I am ever let out of this place, what would I do? I would want to take him with me. I would want to keep him as my pet.

There's no message from Arash on the toilet door. I don't let myself think about what might be happening to him. It gives the interrogators pleasure to break strong people. Probably they admire the strong ones here in a way; admire and detest them. The strong ones, at least, give them a challenge. Those like me must disgust them. No resistance.

I drink water from the sink tap, as Sohrab told me I must. He thinks the water is okay to drink. From Sohrab, I get the advice of an expert. He knows how the whole of Evin works. He knows when the shifts change, and what guards will be working at a certain time of day, what their weaknesses are, how short their tempers are, whether they're lazy or diligent. On top of that, he has a story to tell – which for me is like a radio serial, a type of entertainment, even though the story is harrowing. Maybe it's more like a soap opera of a different sort. I notice that he is not all that interested in my story. He has asked me a little about how I came to be here but, so far as I can tell, he thinks my story is pretty much run-of-the-mill.

For a moment, I find myself wishing that it was Arash in the cell above me instead of Sohrab, because Arash knows me from the outside world. He knows the normal me, not just the Zarah who spends so much time crying. How wonderful it would be to hear his voice coming down through the grille, calm and comforting, and always with that note of amused disdain for his enemies! He could be only a short distance from me right now; two cells away; three. I can imagine his will and resolve, which he never brags about, seeping down to me, reviving me, so that when the guard comes to take me for interrogation I could smile sardonically and mutter something like, 'Another glorious day in Evin!' and walk out of the cell with my shoulders square and my head held high. Or am I romanticising Arash? Perhaps he is as frightened as I am. Perhaps he yearns for an Arash of his own.

But I shouldn't be thinking in this way. How would I cope without Sohrab? I tell myself that if I can't be strong and brave, I can at least be faithful. But I want to be faithful to Arash, too.

On the way back to the cell, a new guard, a woman, surprises me with a question.

'How old are you?'

I turn my head towards this new woman, even though I can't see her through my blindfold. I know she isn't the one who intervened when I was being beaten. She sounds as if she might be forty or more, but it's very difficult to tell. When she asked me how old I was, it wasn't a demand; it wasn't harsh at all. Why should she care? Is it that I look about eighty in some ways, and she is curious about the way in which being here in her lovely workplace has aged me?

'Twenty,' I tell her.

She is walking more closely behind me than the other guards do. I don't like it.

'Want a cigarette?' she asks me.

'No. I don't smoke.'

'Something else, maybe? What would you like? Some nice

soap? Would you like some nice soap?'

'No, I don't want any soap. Thank you.'

'What, then? I can get it.'

'Can you call my mum?'

'Call your mum? No. Something else.'

'If you can call my mum, that would be the best thing I could ask you for. Please will you do that?'

I've stopped walking and have turned around to face her.

'No, not that. But I can give you something that would make you forget about your mum. I can do that.'

'I don't need anything,' I say, and turn away and start shuffling my way forward again. The woman catches up to me and walks by my side. She puts her hand on my shoulder. She is not restraining me. She is attempting to be friendly.

'Think about it,' she says. 'I will be in tomorrow, too.'

'I don't want anything. I don't want anything, tomorrow or ever.'

'Don't say that. That's bad to say. Wait till tomorrow. You'll change your mind.'

Back in my cell, I take a few minutes to think about what the new guard has been saying to me. I think of a number of motives she might have. She might be trying to trap me, so that she can accuse me of trying to bribe her. Perhaps the interrogators have told her to trap me like that. Or is it possible that she is just being kind? Are there such people here in Evin?

I call up to Sohrab, 'Are you there?'

I hear a short laugh. 'No,' he says. 'I've gone for a walk in the garden.'

I tell Sohrab about the new guard, and what she offered me. I tell him I'm perplexed. Does he know what she is on about?

'Did you accept?' he asks me.

'I don't smoke. But it's odd, isn't it? I didn't know that you can get things like that here — cigarettes, soap. She knows I don't have any money.'

'She doesn't want money.'

'She doesn't want money? Are you telling me she's working for charity? Tell me!'

'She wants to sleep with you,' he says calmly.

'No!'

'Yes.'

'I'm so ugly!' I say, amazing myself by thinking of this first. Vanity lasts a long, long time after there is nothing to be vain about.

'She might be uglier.'

'Is that why she touched me?'

'Did she actually touch you?' Surprise has come into his voice.

'Not like that. Just on my shoulder for a few seconds.'

'You're a child. Did you ask for anything?'

'Yes, but she said she can't do it.'

'What did you want?'

'I wanted her to call my mum. I wanted her to tell my mum that I'm okay. She says she can't.'

'Zarah, you have no brains. You know, they were right to lock you up in here. You're too stupid to walk about the streets.'

It is very rare for my madman to call me by my name. It touches me deeply. I feel like stroking his face, my madman's face.

'She asked me if I wanted anything, so I told her. Is that so bad?'

'Listen to me. Don't talk to them anymore. Don't say anything to them. When they ask if you want anything, keep your lips together. Don't say anything rude; just say nothing. If you make a deal, they'll come to your cell and rape you. They want you to make a deal. That's how it starts. Are you listening to me, idiot?'

'Okay, okay.'

All at once, I feel sick with exhaustion. I can't be expected to keep guessing the motives of these people! My brain wanted to believe that the new guard was different. I wanted her to be a kind guard, somebody more like the human beings I've known most of my life. But no, it appears I'm not allowed the great luxury of a little bit of hope. First that fat, stinky bastard, and now the new guard. Well, I never hoped for anything from Stinky, but I did want the new guard to be a good person. Against the odds. It would have meant so much.

I lie down with my blanket over me and try to weep, but no tears come. My own tear ducts don't have any sympathy with my stupidity. It's as if they're saying, 'We'll save ourselves for something less foolish.' I make the sounds of weeping, but it's useless.

'Sohrab?' I call.

'What is it?'

'Thank you for telling me. Thank you for that.'

He gives his gurgling little laugh, then no more than ten seconds pass before he begins moaning.

'Oh, for heaven's sake!' I mutter, and lie listening to Sohrab shrieking, 'Leila! You bitch, Leila! God knows, if I ever get out of here I'll break your neck!'

—

It's early morning. Dawn prayer has just finished. It's cold, and I have my smelly blanket drawn up to my neck and wrapped tightly around my body. I listen to the prison sounds. First come the footfalls of a guard walking along the corridor alone; it's the limping guard – I know his irregular signature. I hear him stop and say something in a very quiet voice, practically a whisper. I don't know if he is talking to himself or to another guard. I hear the remote, weeping sound that's there all the time, and as always I try to work out if the weeping is that of a real person or something piped in to get on the nerves of the prisoners – the muzak of the interrogators. It's strange, but even though the weeping sound goes on all the time, it's possible to not hear it and imagine that there is complete silence. Then, just when I think, *Nothing is happening, nothing is moving,* I realise that the weeping sound is still there, and has been since I started listening.

I hear doors opening and doors closing. My hearing is so acute now that I can tell whether a door opening or closing is on this floor, or the floor above, or the floor below, and whether it is at the end of a corridor, or halfway along, or at the top of some steps – in which case it echoes. I can even tell if it is a door I have passed through. I have built up a sound library in my head of squeaks and creaks and scrapes. And so I suppose I can't say that my time in Evin has been totally wasted. I have improved my hearing.

A trolley is being pushed along the corridor of the floor above – Sohrab's floor. If I asked him about it, I know what he'd say: 'Tea and cakes.' I will save that sound up to give him the chance to be funny. Oh, and isn't that another thing the Evin Academy has taught me? To be provident.

Just for the moment, I'm not conscious of any pain in my body. There's a lulling feeling all over me. I'm even free for now of the need to scratch my scalp. In this time before full consciousness returns to my brain, I indulge myself in a fantasy

I've developed over the past few days. It's an escape fantasy. It's impossible to escape from Evin, or that is what is said on the outside, and now that I'm inside I have no doubt at all that what is said is perfectly true. It's a fortress, it's immense, and it's said to be guarded with every type of electronic device, not to mention God-knows-how-many soldiers, but I can get a little cheap enjoyment out of such daydreams.

My escape fantasy is not like my murder fantasies, which demand a fully alert brain. The escape fantasy is a movie I've put together; and while the murder fantasies always leave me quivering with self-disgust, the escape movie makes me happy, and there's no disgust to deal with. I think the two sorts of fantasy feed very different appetites. There's no doubt that homicide and revenge is the dirtier fantasy, and the more important one. The sickness in me that it exploits is precious to me, I must confess.

I press the switch and run my happy escape movie in my head. In the opening scene, I am lying here exactly where I am. I hear the sounds of gunfire and shouting. Guards call out to other guards in panic. Then, pow! – a loud explosion. I get to my feet, certain that something stupendous is unfolding. I hear the rapid sounds of automatic weapons' fire, and much more shouting. Pow! A flash of orange light shines for a second through the gap at the bottom of the cell door. I include in my movie glorious, swelling music, like Wagner, or Mahler, or somebody who makes music for Hollywood films. So gorgeous! Oh, my God, the shouting is so close to my cell now! People are trying to rescue me! I scream out, 'I'm here!' I must arm myself, in case I have to join in the fighting. I find two pistols in the corner of my cell. They have been concealed all this time by – by whom? I don't know, but they are there. And a great big hammer, too.

But now — Oh heaven! — can it be? I hear Arash's voice, and also that of my father. Bam! The door of my cell is blasted open. Arash stands there, dressed in jeans and the denim shirt I always liked. He hugs me with all his might. 'Follow me!' he says, and I hold tight to the tail of his shirt as he sprints down the corridor, firing his rifles and pistols and all of that, and I'm firing mine, too, although not actually at anyone. My dad is holding the door at the end of the corridor open for me. He is crying and laughing at the same time. 'Wait!' I tell Arash. 'We must get Sohrab!' Arash just laughs. 'Don't worry, we thought of that,' he says. And, sure enough, there stands Sohrab beside me. He looks like Charlie Chaplin.

Now we are out in the street, jumping into a car to drive to the airport. Oh, no! The stinky interrogator is chasing us with a huge gun, really a sort of cannon. I aim my gun at him; but before I can pull the trigger, Stinky blows up. A bomb must have hit him, or something like that. We drive to the airport, Dad and me and Sohrab and Arash and Mum, too. That's the end, driving to the airport.

I make critical comments all through the escape movie. 'How did Arash get out of his cell? Where did his guns come from? And what on earth are those pistols and the hammer doing in your cell? Honestly! Another thing: why does Sohrab look like Charlie Chaplin? That's ridiculous.' If I actually saw such a movie as the one I've made up, I'd smirk scornfully all the way through. I have a friend in the outside world who makes movies, superb movies that are never given a release certificate in Iran. I'd be ashamed to tell him the sort of movies I've been imagining. But even so, the thing I like about the fantasies is that I bother with them at all. If I fantasise about escape, then I haven't become a zombie, have I?

Olives and bread appear under my door on a plastic plate. I sit cross-legged and eat greedily, like a dog that keeps a jealous eye out for any other creature that might try to steal her meal. At the end of eating, my brain is properly awake. Fear has uncoiled itself all through me, from my chest down to my toes. The happiness of the escape movie is far, far away now. I am in a state of readiness for whatever these bastards have waiting for me. But by 'readiness' I don't mean ready to resist or ready to gather up all my courage. I mean ready to scream, ready to beg. I asked Sohrab the other day about the special place that is rumoured to exist within Evin. In the outside world it was mentioned in whispers, black whispers, and was sometimes made the subject of macabre jokes. It is said to have been set up by the SAVAKIs. In 1979, the students who supported the Ayatollah's revolution stormed Evin and displayed the instruments and devices used by SAVAK in this ultimate torture chamber. They were beyond speaking about, beyond writing about. The story goes, though, that when the men of the Ayatollah's new regime took power, they shot or hanged the SAVAKI bosses, but they kept the torturers, the hands-on people, recognising that their skills would be valuable in the coming era. And so it proved, according to the whispers.

Sohrab said, 'Yes, it is there.' And he spoke of it a little more, without dread, because he is mad and far beyond dread.

It is there.

And what good can ever come from people who keep such a place? It appears to be the first place that tyrants think of creating once they have the whip hand; the tyrants of my own land, the tyrants of a hundred others. Such a place is not just a room in a prison; it is a room in a nation.

If I am taken to the special place, I will bargain at every step on the way to its door. 'Whose name do you want?' I will say. 'What do you want me to do?' Even if the bargain only amounts to an agreement to be shot in the back of the head, I will greedily accept. Or if that is not possible – if, when it comes to the moment, there are things I will not do, people I will not betray; if I find something buried deep within me, something I have never seen, never heard from, some ultimate strength – then let the light and love of my mother's God combine with the light and love of my father's God, and let my life rush from me and be gone forever.

It is still early when the guard drops the blindfold through the slot in the door. I have never been taken for interrogation this early in the morning.

'I'm going,' I whisper to Sohrab. I've heard him moving and I know he's awake, but he says nothing.

The guard opens the door and puts what I know to be a chador on my head without saying a word to me. I hate it. It reminds me of those role-playing games I engaged in for Behnam. And why do I have to wear this? What is special about today? Is some big shot scheduled to interrogate me today, some revered holy man? Maybe Khamenei himself? It wouldn't surprise me.

'Where are we going?' I ask the guard, not expecting an answer that means anything.

'Keep walking.'

We stop after just a few seconds. I hear the scraping and wheezing sound of a lift. I recall that sound from when I was first brought to Evin. I hear the 'ding, ding' sound as the lift reaches this floor, and the hiss and groan as the doors open.

The guard pushes me forward. I feel the different surface under my bare feet. I hear the groan of the door closing and feel the sudden lurch as the lift begins to move. I can't tell if we are going up to a higher floor, or down. At first I think we are ascending; then, no, I'm certain we are descending; then I lose all idea.

I can't control my fear. Just this one change to the routine, and I am already half-insane.

'Please tell me where you're taking me. Please tell me.'

'I don't know. No more questions.'

I take a deep breath to prevent myself fainting. I thought I was used to every kind of fear that this place can provide, but this is a new sort. I want to run and throw myself headlong against something hard. The guard can see or sense how the fear is mounting in me, and he takes my wrist and holds it tight.

I hear the 'ding, ding' sound again. We must have descended, because the lift has been in motion too long for us to have been heading upwards. Evin is big, but it is not ten storeys high. We must be deep, deep down.

The guard pulls on my wrist to get me out of the lift, but I won't budge. My immobility is partly will and partly petrification. I know that when they hang someone here, they do it straight after morning prayer. And when they hang a woman, they put a full chador on her head. I have seen hanged women on television. Every Iranian has seen them.

I cling with my free hand to a niche I have found – a part of the door, I think. I hold on with all my strength, and scream my head off.

'Move!' says the guard. 'I don't know where they're taking you. Transferring you to another place. Just move!'

The guard must think this will calm me. It doesn't.

'I don't want to go anywhere!' I shriek. 'I don't want to! Take me back to my cell!'

The guard slaps me hard on the shoulder, then braces my head and slaps at my face. I can't hold to the door any longer. My fingers lose their grip.

'You made me do that!' the guard shouts at me. 'I didn't want to! You forced me, stupid girl!'

We walk for what feels like more than a minute, even more than two. Then the guard makes me stop and stand still. He puts a hand on each of my shoulders and makes me more upright. It is as if he is shaping me, making me more presentable. I hear a door opening, then a rush of fresh air. This is an open area. I can feel the broadness of the space before me through the chador.

Where is this? Where? It's outside, but it's not the street; I'm sure of that. Surely this is the back of Evin, below the mountains of North Tehran. I can hear birdsong. I stop breathing in order to hear the birds.

A car door opens. The sound is distinctive. The guard says, 'Bend your knees,' and I do, without any resistance. He pushes me into the car. I brush against a figure already seated within, then the guard urges me along the seat and climbs in himself, so that I am wedged between two people. My feeling is that the other figure is that of a woman. I have heard no voice, but I feel it is so.

A person in front of me – the driver or someone else – begins talking as soon as the car is in motion. He is responding to someone's voice, but the guard beside me and the person I think is a woman are not saying a thing. This must be a telephone conversation on a mobile. I can't work out the sense of what is being said. It sounds like gibberish or a play language.

The car has been moving for more than five minutes. I know how much time is passing because I am counting in my head. Why I should be doing this, I have no idea. Am I trying to calm myself? How could I possibly believe that I could calm myself! I feel furious with whatever foolish part of me is trying to calm me down! And yet, all through my objections, I continue to count, and I am up to my fourth count of sixty. Oh, but I'm counting too quickly! I slow the count, absurdly, and say beneath my breath, 'One star blink blink, two stars blink blink, three stars blink blink …'

I hear no traffic sounds. Is it possible that the hidden part of Evin is so vast that a car is required to move people about? The guard I imagine to be female shows that she is indeed female by tutting and fussing with my chador, making it sit properly on my hairless skull. I permit her to do it. Why not? It's a task she adores. She's one of those women who gets into a high state of excitement by stopping girls in the street and commanding them to straighten their headscarves. 'God detests a creature who shows her hair to strangers,' she would lecture, because that is exactly what they say. 'Are you prepared for what hell is like?' I know her type so well; I know how proud she is of her job.

chapter twenty-two

B y the end of the war with Iraq, the wail of the Red Alert siren in Tehran, warning of a missile attack, came to be greeted with a shrug of the shoulders by children like me. After all, for many of us, war was normal. The siren would sound, and children would continue to play in the streets, ride their bikes, joke, and skylark. When a missile exploded close by, the boys (and a few girls, too) would grin at each other and say, 'Ha ha, missed!' I would have stayed in the streets playing after the red siren; but, out of concern for my mother, who would have had a heart attack, I always left with Mum and my brothers and sisters for the air-raid shelter, carrying my little case. Inside the case I kept my pyjamas, my coloured pencils, and a colouring book.

People from all over our neighbourhood were down in the tunnels, sheltering from the missiles. The lights were dim, but you could see. Bedding was laid out, and the smallest children were made to curl up under the blankets and at least pretend to sleep, no matter what time it was in the world above. The tunnels were full of the racket of mothers shouting to their older, more unruly kids, and of kids themselves joking and laughing and generally continuing on with the games they had just left. Many people prayed, too, and the unhurried, rhythmic chanting blended in with shrieks and oaths and shrill laughter, and the cries of mothers pleading for some order: 'As God is my judge, I'll take you by your neck and turn your bottom scarlet!'

I sat quietly and plied my coloured pencils. Here was a goblin breaking into a room in which a peasant family was hiding – a great theme of Iranian folk tales. Here was a princess picking flowers in the meadow. Here was Rustam, calling on Sohrab to lay down his sword and depart in peace. Here was a hunter in the age of Darius aiming his arrow at a rearing lion. Other colouring books – not amongst my favourites – gave children the opportunity to do their very best work on the outline of the Ayatollah Khomeini smiling at pious children bowed in prayer.

Above me, as I knew, infernos were devouring houses and people. Soldiers were running this way and that, trying to clear the streets for the fire engines to race through. Naughty boys were ducking down alleys and between piles of smoking debris, lapping up the excitement. Dogs were barking in panic, scouring the streets for their owners. Ambulances were blaring their way to places where people were screaming for help. And there would surely be an old man who felt he had seen too much of fire and death in his life, shaking his fist at the sky or at fate. Just as surely, there would be an old woman, her wits scrambled, shuffling through the chaos as she called the name of her cat. I had seen all this more than once when the red siren sounded a little too late. It didn't distress me to know what was happening above. I was taking great care to stay inside the lines as I concentrated on the figure of the mighty Rustam calling to the young man Sohrab, whom he was not to know was his beloved son. Rustam and Sohrab – that was tragedy. The chaos above – that was a nuisance.

Twelve years later, in my second year at university, I again had the opportunity to either stay in the streets, where crowds were shouting and shaking their fists, or retreat to a shelter. This time, my mother was not able to demand that I come with her to the tunnels with my small suitcase and something to occupy me. This time, I did what I had wished to do all those years earlier when I first became blasé about what might kill me: I stayed in the streets, with no fear of the enemy.

I was ecstatic; what was happening seemed to me unstoppable. The protests had only a very local objective – to demand the reinstatement of a university professor who'd been arrested by the police for teaching in a way that was considered subversive by the Ministry for Education – but we were getting a lot of support from the general public and from some of the bolder newspapers. It seemed to me, and to most of my fellow protestors, that the sheer justice of what we were demanding had disarmed the regime politically; that they were scared, unable to look us in the eye and say that we were in the wrong. After twenty years in power, the regime was exhausted, so we believed. This conviction was foolish, of course, as I came to see. Those in power were simply waiting to see how much force would be required to shut us up – a little or a lot. They had tried a little, it hadn't worked, and they were getting ready to try a lot.

I looked about and saw so many young men and young women, just like me, laughing in the face of the enemy – the enemy this time being the police, the security agents, the stupid boys of the Basij with their pimples and bad breath and brain-dead fanaticism, the mullahs, the rulers, the nation's most practised liars and hypocrites. Harm me? Really? No, they would not harm me, and they would not harm my friends. A great force for reform billowed the sail of our ship. Woe betide those who crossed our bow! There I stood, my scarf thrown back and the wind in my hair, and beside me was Rustam – the Lion himself, the man who made the earth shudder when he lifted his foot and brought it down on the ground. And Rustam's name was Arash.

Then, one day in autumn, I was walking home from university with my books in my bag, and my scarf worn to reveal a rebellious few centimetres of my dark hair. I had just left two of my girlfriends, both of them dauntless firebrands like myself. We'd been discussing the recent student arrests, and talking of how we would call a rally for the next day right within the precincts of the university to protest this blatantly illegal violation of our rights to put our point-of-view. We'd also discussed boyfriends, and had enjoyed ten minutes of the tittering and giggling that Iranian girls so relish in the absence of boys; tittering and giggling that would look to a Western girl painfully teenagerish – but which was, in its way, deadly serious.

With not a thought in my head but of the fine figure I made striding along with my hair showing and my chin held high, I was suddenly alarmed by a car, a green Peugeot, that seemed likely to run me down, as well it might because I was walking down the very middle of the street. I was preparing to say something like, 'Hey, watch it, brother!' but never got the chance. A woman in a police uniform stepped out of the car and rapidly demanded to see my identity papers. Within a further minute, and even before my identity papers had been properly studied, I was in the back of the car with the woman officer on one side of me and a male police officer on the other side. A third policeman was driving. I wrenched my head around to see if my friends had noticed what had happened. They were both running down the street after the car; but, with a couple of seconds of acceleration, the driver left them well behind.

I knew that I was possibly in the worst kind of trouble; that this sort of swoop by the police could end badly for me. I'd heard of other student protestors being grabbed off the street in this way, and being beaten black and blue and then dumped in some remote suburb in the middle of the night. But this hadn't happened all that often, and never to anyone I knew well. I'd thought that if the police took an interest in me they would make an appointment, and ask me a few questions that I'd answer curtly and then go home. I hadn't believed that my life could be invaded by people I considered beneath me. A cloak of snobbishness, as I came to see, was what I'd relied on for protection.

And now, absurdly, I continued to trust in this snobbishness. 'Excuse me,' I said. 'Where am I being taken, and for what reason?'

'The station,' said the woman, without looking at me. 'We have some questions for you to answer.' Her tone wasn't harsh; it was perhaps more bored than anything.

'Questions about what matter?'

'You'll be told.'

'I wish to be told now.'

The woman ignored me. The male officer smiled – quite aware, I think, that my composure was fake.

I was preparing another question when the driver stopped the car. The woman officer produced a blindfold and slipped it over my head and my scarf, and patted it with her fingers until it sat firmly over my eyes. In the darkness, I had already begun the long and agonising process of repentance for everything I had ever done that could possibly give offence to people such as these in the car with me. It was a process of repenting and recanting.

Oh, God, what have I done? I'm going to apologise as soon as they ask me to. I'll fall to my knees. I'll promise to never ever do anything bad again. But how dare they! Yes, how dare they! I have done nothing wrong. I'll demand to be released or I'll take my story to the newspapers. Honestly, do they think they're dealing with some peasant from the sticks? Oh, my mother. Dear God, my mother! She'll die. She'll never be able to bear this! I'm going to tell them that I didn't know what I was doing. I was sucked into the whole thing. I had bad friends; they misled me. I'm too young to know my own mind. But Arash — what would he think? He'll be so ashamed of me. He'll disown me. He'll pretend that he understands why I pleaded with the cops; but, really, he'll be disappointed. Well, you know what? There'll be no pleading from me! None! This is illegal, what they're doing — illegal! Dear God, don't they pay policemen enough for them to buy deodorant? Phew! And her, too. Dad will get me a lawyer. It'll be okay.

I heard traffic sounds as we were driving, but not very distinctly. I had no idea where I was being taken. I doubted that I was going to a police station. There are police stations everywhere in Tehran; they could have reached one in sixty seconds. But if not to a police station, then where?

With each passing minute, my mouth became drier. I wouldn't have enough moisture in my mouth to plead; certainly not enough to rage.

The car finally slowed, made a sharp turn, then stopped.

The woman officer nudged me. 'Move,' she said — once again, not harshly.

The woman officer followed behind me with a hand on my shoulder. I hadn't worn a blindfold since I was a kid playing games with other kids. I remembered the delicious, scary thrill of those games, with my friends shrieking, 'Zarah! Zarah! You're going over a cliff! Watch out!' Now it was different. There was no glee in my fear. I imagined a club raised, ready to strike me, or a fist. I was panting like a cat when it's terrified, my heart beating so fast it felt as if it would fly into pieces. I could hear twittering, like that of birds in a big cage, except that the twittering was human. The woman officer said, 'Stop.' I stood still as I was commanded. I tried to make my stillness seem exemplary, as if to show that I was really a good girl who could follow orders. I felt baffled as I tried to imagine what was going on around me. People brushed against me, as if they were busily on their way to somewhere. I heard laughter, and I heard a booming, male voice demanding that the laughter cease.

The woman officer pulled the blindfold away, but left the chador in place. It took only a few seconds for me to realise that I was in a big detention centre. A number of police officers were standing about looking jaded, but others were busy at their desks writing on documents or recording information from a pair of young women who stood at the counter. My first thought, other than being intensely aware of my sense of dread, was: *Why do policemen always look so unhealthy? Don't they ever eat vegetables and fruit?*

A woman officer – not the one who was guarding me – started shrieking at the women and girls slouched against the concrete walls of the place. She made gestures with her hands as if she were trying to make a whole lot of chickens hasten along before her. The women and girls gathered around me. I was still standing like a statue, barely daring to move my eyelids, when I realised that they were all prostitutes, even the very young ones. They would have been gathered up in the big sweeps of the city that the cops and Basij militia carried out all through the day and night, and they would have been brought here to be fined or imprisoned. I said, 'Good afternoon to you,' to those closest to me, but they only looked at me and grinned contemptuously. 'Another uni bird,' one of them said to her neighbour.

The women were quite argumentative. Actually, all Iranians are argumentative nearly all the time, but these women hadn't suspended their bad habits just because they were in custody.

They demanded to know why they'd been arrested, even though it was obvious. 'How about me?' one girl said. 'What am I supposed to have done?' She was wearing a pair of shorts. Another one pointed at her lips and said, 'It's not lipstick. I had a lolly.' The other girls laughed at her story, and she even started laughing at it herself. Oh, God, how I wished I was one of them, one of these bold women! I'd have been happy to have shared their punishment; happy to have shared a cell with any of them, for a year if necessary. At least they knew what they faced; they'd probably all been through it before. But I knew only that I was either in big trouble or in even-worse-than-big trouble.

The female officer who'd been in the Peugeot with me got sick of waiting, and went off, muttering that she had better things to do than stand around all day. I remained standing perfectly still, not even prepared to shift my weight from foot to foot in case it was taken as a sign of insolence. The women around me obviously thought I was a sissy. They shook their heads and made little snorts of derisive laughter.

Finally, the officer with the booming voice came over to us and motioned with his hands for all of us to move it. On the far side of the detention room a tall, wire gate was rolled open and we were hustled inside. Then the gate was drawn shut and locked. The other women, expecting boredom, looked for ways to make themselves slightly more comfortable – lounging against the walls, leaning against each other shoulder-to-shoulder – but I continued to stand there in my obedient, upright way. When I saw that hardly any of the cops were paying attention to us, I risked speaking to one of the women.

'Will you ring my mum when you get out?' I whispered. 'I'd be very, very grateful. Please will you ring her and tell her I've been arrested?'

The woman, far from young when I looked at her close up, shook her head unhurriedly.

'You're a political,' she said. 'If I do something for you, I'm in the shit.'

'Please. I have a little bit of money. I'll give it to you.'

'No.'

She wandered away from me, but I shuffled after her and caught her up, all the time looking over my shoulder.

'Do you know what's going to happen?' I asked her. 'Can you tell me that, at least?'

She didn't look at me at first, then she risked a glance. 'Evin,' she said.

'Are you sure?'

'You asked me, little sister, so I'm telling you.'

I wanted to ask more, but the woman moved away again.

I thought, *God, please protect me!*

I took up my statue position again, and waited. My heartbeat had slowed, probably as a result of standing so still for two hours, but now it began racing again. Standing still didn't help this time. My brain felt as if walls within it were withering away like paper held close to a flame. Thoughts that were normally kept separate were running together. But my one clear thought, the one that resisted the chaos around it, was simply, *I don't have the strength for this.*

chapter twenty-three

Once I am out of the car, the male officer guides me by prodding me in the small of the back every two steps. I am so used to walking in my blindfold that I have developed a radar-like way of seeing what's around me. I have no way of confirming my guesses, but I feel that I would be right if I could suddenly see. Right now, I feel certain that a large building is before me; and, sure enough, I hear the rasp of sliding doors a second before the balm of artificially cooled air wraps itself around my body.

I am prodded forward for quite some distance once within the building. I imagine a vast foyer dwarfing me in its capaciousness. I hear echoing footsteps. The surface beneath my bare feet puzzles me. It is not concrete; it is harder than concrete, which has a surprisingly resilient feel once you get used to walking on it sightlessly. No, this is more like tile, or some sort of stone. I guard against relaxing my fear, but it does seem that I am in a huge office block; a ministry, perhaps, rather than a dungeon deep in the earth with a scaffold waiting. They will not hang me here, although I may be here for the preliminaries to a hanging.

I am manoeuvred around a corner, and around another. Something brushes against my shoulder; something that bends. Foliage? An indoor plant? A door opens, and I pass through. I am moving rapidly, much more rapidly than along the corridors of Evin. My feeling is that business is to be transacted; everything about this experience has the air of briskness.

The officer tells me to stop and stand still. For a moment, I suspect a trick. A sickly taste of bile comes into my mouth. Have I deceived myself? Am I actually facing a firing squad? But then the officer deftly slips off my blindfold and, after blinking against the bright overhead lighting, I see that I am indeed in some sort of office building, and that I am facing a door with a plaque fixed to it. The plaque hasn't been attached properly; it is a little higher on one side than the other. What is written on the plaque makes no sense; I think it is a misspelling of 'Do not enter'. The officer moves slightly ahead of me in order to open the door, and I have my first look at this person who has been sitting beside me in the car and prodding me in the back. He is neither tall nor short, and completely unremarkable in every other way, too; not good-looking, not ugly, not even plain; just very ordinary.

The door opens and I am staring ahead at what appears to be a management suite: a table with a smooth surface of artificial woodgrain; plastic chairs with metal legs; large portraits on the wall of Khomeini and Khamenei, the father of the nation and his successor, with identical mullah's turbans, identical white beards.

A tall man in a dark suit with an open-collared shirt is standing beside the table looking at me over the top of his glasses, which sit halfway down his nose. Although he is young — maybe twenty-seven or twenty-eight — he is important looking, just as he wishes to appear, I have no doubt. To his right sits a young woman at a desk with her fingers working at a computer keyboard. She glances at me for a half-second without any interest. There is another man in the room sitting to the left of Mr Important. He's older, middle-aged, and for some reason I feel I've seen him before. Where? I can't bring the occasion to mind. The older man doesn't even bother to look at me. I'm staring down at the nails of my bare feet, where a tiny amount of pink nail-polish remains. It was my little nephew who painted my nails pink. It was a great project for him; a happy project, with a little bit of wickedness mixed in.

'Have a seat, sister,' says Mr Important, and as he speaks he takes a seat himself behind the smooth desk and makes a motion with his hand for the officer to leave. I move a short distance to a row of brown plastic chairs, and sit on the closest one with my hands folded on my lap. Mr Important opens a folder and bends forward to read from it. The woman at the computer keeps her fingers poised above the keyboard. The older man, the one who is familiar to me, looks away to one side, studying nothing at all.

These people are in no hurry. The briskness I was aware of before has diminished.

Perhaps ten minutes pass before a knock sounds on the door behind me.

'Yes, come in,' says Mr Important, looking up from the folder.

The door opens. I turn my head just a fraction. It is my interrogator, Stinky. The sight of him instantly triggers a reaction of sickness and disgust in me. My hand goes up to my face involuntarily, as if I am preparing for a blow.

'Good morning to you, Haji,' he says, addressing Mr Important. He puts his hands together in the prayer position and gives a small bow in the direction of the older man, but doesn't address him in words. 'Sorry for the delay,' says Stinky, and he seats himself two chairs along from me. A whiff of some sort of scent reaches my nostrils. Stinky has freshened himself up with cologne! The scent that disguises his vile smell is very like the good manners he pretends to have around other people.

With the arrival of Stinky, a dangerous reaction has sprung up in me. At first it was hatred and disgust, but what is happening now is far worse, for I feel that I might suddenly stand and spit on him. I am horrified at what I am imagining, but I don't feel confident that I can regain control of myself. I drop my head to my chest, squeeze my eyes tightly shut, and hiss silently at this demon who has jumped into my brain: 'Stop it! Stop it!'

I become aware of a sound quite close by, and open my eyes. The older man has leaned forward and is tapping the surface of the table with the tips of his fingers.

'Face this way,' he says. His voice carries the crackle of menace, and I obey.

The demon in my head has gone.

Mr Important clears his throat and begins to speak, or really to chant, for he is speaking in formal Arabic and in the manner of a mullah: 'In the name of Allah who will forgive us for whatever mistakes we make, and his prophet Mohammad, and his Book Koran, which will guide us to His promised heaven.'

These words are used on many formal occasions in Iran, always as an introduction to something official. I understand for the first time why I am here today. This is a court. I have heard these words spoken on televised reports from Revolutionary Courts. Is that where I have seen this older man?

The woman at the computer takes over from Mr Important, reading from her computer screen. Her voice is very sing-song, and she has an irritating way of extending the final syllable of the word at the end of each sentence.

'Zarah Ghahramani, translating student, Faculty of Languages, Allame Tehran, entered in the Year of the Prophet, 1377. Born in the Year of the Prophet, 1360, thirty-first day of Shahrivar. Birth certificate number 843. Is this you?'

I nod my head.

The woman, who appears to have more authority than I thought at first, asks shrilly, 'Is this you?'

'Yes,' I answer.

She looks back to the screen of her computer and starts reading again.

'You have been charged with numbers of offences. I will now summarise these offences. One, deranging the university environment and making it uncomfortable for other students and teachers. Two, encouraging other students to cancel classes on a number of occasions. Three, writing articles critical of the government of the Islamic Republic of Iran and questioning the government's policies in different areas. Four, delivering speeches on the grounds and within the buildings, classrooms, and offices of the university protesting the valid judgements of the Revolutionary Supreme Court in regard to judgements handed down in the cases of accused fellow students. Five, encouraging students at the university to lie down in the streets, so causing tension between students and the police. Six, conducting an illegal and immoral sexual relationship with fellow accused Arash Hazrati.'

She stops there and looks in the direction of Mr Important.

Nothing is said for a short time. What I want to say is, 'So what?', but of course I say nothing. Then I realise that everyone is waiting for me to speak. I don't know what I could say that would please them. Maybe, 'Guilty. Horribly guilty. Disgustingly guilty.'

Mr Important is staring at me. 'Miss Ghahramani, do you accept that you have committed these offences?' he asks.

I don't say anything.

'Miss Ghahramani, you have already been found guilty of the charges brought against you. Do you accept that you have committed these offences?'

'Do you mean that I have been to court already? Do you mean that I have been tried?' I try to ask these questions in a casual way, but a certain amount of anger creeps into my tone.

'We are only announcing the result of your trial to you,' says Mr Important. 'Your guilt was well established.'

'Who were my accusers? Who said that I did these things?'

Again, the anger.

Mr Important seems to be exercising patience. He scratches his temple before answering.

'Your accusers were the Revolutionary Court and the Public Representative. All legal requirements have been strictly observed.'

'Did I have a lawyer?'

'Oh, yes. You had a very good lawyer. Your lawyer was Arash Hazrati. You would consider him a good lawyer, wouldn't you, Miss Ghahramani?'

He looks at me with a little smile, and I notice that the older man has allowed himself to smile, too.

The demon is now well and truly back inside my skull. 'Fuck you and fuck your court!' is what I would say if I had the madness and courage of Sohrab. I drop my head to my chest, and mouth these words rapidly, making it look as though I am praying.

'I have nothing to say' is the only response I make.

The woman with the irritating voice takes her cue and starts chanting the words on her screen once again: 'In the name of Allah, accused Zarah Ghahramani has been found guilty according to evidence recorded during interrogations. Accused will spend thirty days in prison, the days already spent in custody to be deducted from the thirty-day sentence. Accused will be deprived of the benefits of university enrolment. Accused will repay funds provided by the state for her education. Accused has acknowledged that she abused the government's generosity and abused the government's budget for education. Accused will not be permitted to re-enrol in her course at her ex-university at any time in the future. Accused will not be permitted to enrol at any university in the Islamic Republic in the future. Accused will not be permitted to take employment with any newspaper or magazine. Accused will not engage in political subversion either by means of speech or by means of writing. Do you have anything to say in your defence?'

I am astonished by the question, but only for a few seconds. I realise that my appearance here is no more than a grotesque formality. In God's name, do I have anything to say in my defence? They ask me this after telling me that my case has already been decided. It is obvious that you can only prosper in a government such as the one that makes the rules in my country if you have practically no sense of the absurd at all.

I mean, amongst my friends, absurdities are seized on and made fun of – even our own. We are embarrassed by them. But these people – my vile interrogator; Mr Important; the older man with the menacing voice; the irritating stooge who sits at the keyboard – they're not in the least embarrassed. It simply doesn't matter to them. I know they say that power corrupts, but they should tell you that the corruption begins with the powerful losing their embarrassment at being ridiculous. Why should they care if you laugh at them? They know that they can make you forget about laughter forever, if they wish. They *own* pain. It is their servant. In the end, although my friends and I would like to believe otherwise, you will get your way much quicker with a cruel servant like pain to carry out your bidding than with a witty servant like laughter.

'No,' I say, staring down at my hands in my lap, and I add, in a whisper, 'Why don't you just kill me?' I am shocked at what I've whispered, and hope with all my heart that it hasn't carried to the ears of these people. I continue to stare at my hands. When I glance up, I can't tell immediately from the expression of Mr Important and the older man if they have heard.

'Your confession will be made public in due course,' says Mr Important. 'God's blessing on all of us.'

It appears that they haven't heard, because Mr Important has closed the folder and looks as if he is ready to move on to some other case. Stinky leaves the room and returns with my blindfold. He slips it over my head and tells me to stand. I hear the older guy say to Stinky, 'God bless you, Haji. I hope I can compensate you one day.' And Stinky replies, 'My duty. No more than my duty, Haji.'

—

Back in my cell in Evin, all the bitterness and anger that I couldn't express in the courtroom seethes in my heart and head. I scratch at my scalp in retaliation for my cowardice. I disgust myself. I should have spat on Stinky. I should have spat on all of them, especially on the woman at the keyboard who, in retrospect, is even more irritating to me than she was at the time. Is it because she is a woman, and she would know what was done to me, and yet knowing it she can sit there and read all that rubbish from her computer screen like the stooge she is? Maybe. Or maybe it's just that she is more my size. If I jumped on her and punched her, I could knock her teeth out with no difficulty at all.

Then I begin to think of what was said at the end of the 'trial'. I think about the older man saying, 'I hope I can compensate you one day' to that cretin. What did that mean? Pacing up and down in the tiny space I have, I try to work it out, but can't. Then, when I have given up, it comes to me, and I stop in my pacing and whisper, 'You bastards!' It was a deal. My interrogator, Stinky, or Gholam, to give him his real name, had delivered me alive, and now the older guy owes him a favour. This is what Behnam's intervention has provided, probably. This is the outcome of various bribes and promises and the scratching of backs: Gholam, who must be a law unto himself, has generously agreed not to go as far as he might have. What did they say to him, the people along this line of favour-givers and bribe-takers? 'Oh, have your fun with her, that's okay, but don't actually kill her if you can avoid it. And the special place, Gholam? You know your special place? Best not take her there.' And, I realise, that's probably where I've seen the older guy – at some gathering of big wheels that I've attended with Behnam.

You bastards!

And what is the fate of those who have no friends in high places? Those who cannot prevail on Gholam to temper his methods? Those who can't pay the money, or can't provide those treats that the people along the line so crave? The new refrigerator, the dishwasher, the gigantic television set, the tickets to Paris? Iran has a punishment market, so it seems, where the torment of a young woman can be traded for a washing machine.

'I thought you were gone for good,' Sohrab calls down to me.

'I went to court.'

'Are you going home?'

'They said I will, but I don't believe it. They said I can't go to uni anymore, and I can't write anymore.'

'Do you write?'

'A little.'

'I wouldn't read it. It'd be rubbish.'

'Why do you say that?'

'I know you people. You think you can make everything beautiful. You think you can make Gholam into a rosebush. What a waste of ink!'

'He smelt like a rosebush today. He came to court.'

'You deceive yourselves. You tell yourselves children's stories. You make me sick.'

'You're in a funny mood!'

'A club comes down on your head and you burst into tears. But you stood right under the club. I despise all of you. I despise you especially.'

'Oh, shut up. Shut up and fuck off.'

'Princess! I've never heard you swear before!'

'Well, get used to it.'

'Say it again.'

'No.'

'The little lamb is turning into a wolf. Well, Evin has done you some good, after all.'

I have nothing to say to Sohrab for the rest of the day. I hate it when he's sarcastic.

I sit on my blanket and try to imagine what sort of life I can have now. I can't study. I can't write. I can be a checkout chick, or something like that. As long as I don't talk to the customers. As long as I don't make any subversive comments about the soap someone is buying, or say that one brand of toothpaste is better than another. As long as I stop thinking altogether and just say, 'Good morning' to everyone, and nothing else. As long as I read nothing except the approved newspapers and magazines full of stories about the wicked enemies of Iran and the wicked things they get up to. Why, do you know, some of these wicked nations that want the revolution of the Iranian people to fail actually torture people? That's right, torture! Oh, they must be very wicked people indeed to do that!

I'm trying to forget that my bladder is full. I know that the new female guard is on duty, the one who wants to sleep with me, according to Sohrab. I shut my eyes and try to imagine that I am a dry sponge, able to soak up litres and litres of water. But it is of no use. I have to put out the green slip.

And she comes to take me to the toilet straight away. She must have been standing out there, waiting for the green slip. Such dedication! She'll go a long way in her career.

'Did you think about what I said?' she asks me as soon as she opens the door.

'I'm not a druggie.'

'Everyone does drugs. Don't be foolish.'

'Well, I don't.'

She takes my hand and holds it as we make our way along the corridor to the toilets. I don't make an issue of it. If I don't get

223

to the toilet soon I am going to pee in my pants. She waits outside the door of the cubicle. I have my blindfold off, which is permitted, so long as you have it back on once you exit. I hate the thought of her listening to me pee, but I can hardly tell her to go away. Usually the guards stand outside the entrance to the toilets, and spare you any embarrassment.

Without warning, the guard pushes the door open and stares down at me. I am too shocked by her appearance to scream; I simply stare back. She's much younger than I'd thought, only about thirty. She's skinny and short, much shorter than me, which is another surprise; I'd thought she was tall. She's obviously from the south — dark complexioned, as many people in the south of Iran are. But the truly shocking thing has nothing to do with her age or height, but with the horrible deformity of her face. It's flattened, as if all the raised features have been burned off or sliced away, then poorly repaired with surgery. She is allowing me to stare. Because of her deformities, it is impossible to tell if she is smiling or scowling.

I've got to my feet and stand before her, probably with horror written all over my face. She reaches forward to take hold of my shoulders, or maybe to embrace me. Even at this moment, I challenge myself to refrain from showing any disgust at her features, but I have no hope. I push forward with my hands using all my strength, knocking her backwards out of the cubicle and off her feet. I run from the toilets into the corridor.

Oh, and here is yet another shock for me, for this is the first time I have seen the corridor with my true vision, rather than my guesswork radar vision. It is far, far bigger than I thought, brightly lit, and all in black and white, with cameras everywhere on the walls, peering down like insects. The corridor I am in runs before me and behind me forever. Hundreds of doors open off it and, at intervals, intersecting corridors head left and right. I am frozen where I stand by the sheer scale of Evin. This is not simply a prison. This huge, swollen fortress for the isolation of killers and thieves and prostitutes and embezzlers and drunkards and protestors is itself a city, with another city surrounding it, and the fortress draws people from the city outside through its gates to fill its cells, as if the stream of the inducted is its lifeblood. My friends are in here somewhere. In a week of searching, how would I find them? I can't even begin to work out the way back to my own cell.

And so I stand where I am, incapable of moving a muscle. The whole place is silent: no shrieking, no sobbing, nothing at all. Now I hear the footsteps of the guard approaching me. I turn and stare at her, at the face that barely exists; the face that reveals nothing except its hideousness. She walks straight up to me and pulls the blindfold over my head. Then she slaps me on the face, and it is a hard slap – hard enough to my make ears ring. Despite the ringing, I can hear someone running towards us.

'What is it, sister?'

It's the voice of a man.

'She pushed me in the toilet and tried to run away. She's lost her senses.'

The man grabs my face and holds it with his fingers digging into my cheeks.

'Little bitch,' he says, and squeezes harder. My lips and nose are bunched together. He starts to pull me down the corridor with my face gripped in his hand, but then seizes my shoulder instead and drags me so rapidly I can barely keep from falling. I hear the sound of my own cell-door opening – I know its sound – before I am thrown through the air, landing half on the floor and half against a wall. The throw has somehow wrenched my blindfold off. The guard kicks me where I lie, aiming for my stomach but not connecting. He heaves me to my feet and punches me while holding me upright. I can't support my weight, and collapse. The guard lets me fall, then bends down over me and beats me with both fists. The blows land on my face, my shoulders, my chest.

Some vestige of my vanity remains, and I writhe to deflect the blows to my face, particularly to my mouth and my teeth. I want to keep my teeth, at least. I can't manage that for very long, and instead struggle to crawl away until I am jammed against the wall with no further place to escape to. The guard keeps drawing back his fist and ramming it into whatever part of me he can reach. My whole body feels like a deep, throbbing bruise on which more and more blows land. In my writhing, I glimpse the female guard standing just outside the cell door watching. If she is gloating, I can't tell. I am trying to plead, but I'm not permitted to finish even one word. The pain is the worst I've ever known.

Then I hear another sound, a shrieking sound that includes my name and a torrent of swear words. It's Sohrab, screaming his lungs out.

The guard steps away from me, heaving to catch his breath. I try to get to my knees, perhaps imagining that I can run away. The guard takes a big step across the cell and is over me again, punching with renewed energy. My last image before I faint is of the female guard at the door. She is standing with both boots together, as if at attention.

I come to with my face flat against the floor. Perhaps only a short time has passed since I fainted. The man who was beating me has gone, I think. I'm trying to raise my head, but can't. Pain is coming from so many parts of me that I am left confused, unable to test any one place with my fingers to see if there is a cut or if any bones are broken. My eyes won't open properly, and what vision I have is blurred by my lashes. Breathing seems to make the pain worse. I try holding my breath, but that's worse still. Something bad is wrong with me.

'Wake up! Talk! Can you hear me?'

Who is that?

'Talk to me! Can you hear me?'

It's Sohrab. I don't even attempt to answer him. He keeps saying the same things over and over. I want him to shut up.

I try a small movement, just onto my side to relieve the pain in my chest. I brace myself for a flood of pain, but it doesn't come — or not in a flood, at least. I lie still and think about my next movement. I lift one hand, wanting to feel if my teeth have been broken, but this movement brings the wave of pain I'd expected before. I pause, then persist. I've tried feeling for my teeth with my tongue, but it doesn't work. I think I have bitten into my tongue, and it hurts too much to make it move. I've got my fingers up to my mouth. I part my lips a little and touch. My teeth are still there.

With tiny movements and wriggles, I've got my body into a position that is the least painful of those I've tried. I can't close my eyes properly, so I settle for a blurry, almost-closed compromise.

Sohrab is still shouting.

'I'm okay,' I try to call out, then have to put my face sideways and let blood ooze out. I get my hand up to my face again, and wipe away the blood from my nose. I can't tell if my mouth is bleeding or if the blood from my nose is running into my mouth. Probably both.

'Talk to me! Can you hear me?'

'I'm okay.'

'Can you hear me?'

I attempt to make Sohrab understand that I'm okay again and again, but I can't make my voice carry to him. Perhaps the words I'm saying sound like moans and groans. So, for how long I don't know, I'm slurring out the words, 'I'm okay,' and Sohrab is shouting down to me, 'Are you okay? Can you hear me?' The whole attempt at communication becomes an added torment to me. Then I hear the door to my cell open, and all the difficulty I have had trying to make a loud sound disappears, and I scream.

The female guard stands outside the door, just as she was standing before I fainted. I can only see her silhouette.

'Would you say no if I was pretty?' she asks.

I can't even begin to find the will to answer her.

'I said, would you say no if I was pretty?'

There is a threat in her voice. I'm trying as hard as I can to say 'No' to her, because I think that might be the right answer.

'I was prettier than you before they bombed our street. I got burned then. My family died. I have no friends.'

Why on earth is she telling me this? Is she insane?

'I would've got you something good. But all you say to me is "No". All you say is "Get away from me!", don't you?'

How in heaven's name does she expect me to reply to her? She has just finished watching the guard beat me black and blue, and now she wants to tell me her life story?

'You think you can pick and choose, don't you? You can't pick and choose in Evin. You're not pretty anymore. You look worse than me. Nobody would want you now. Not even Gholam would want you now.'

She's crying, I think. Her voice is shaking.

'I hope they keep you here forever,' she says. 'When you beg me for something to kill yourself with, I will have nothing for you. You're like all the others. I hate all of you.'

She remains standing there, crying. Or, if she's not crying, she must be trembling with rage. I can see her outline shaking. I don't feel sorry for her, if that's what she's hoping. I want her to drop dead.

She shuts the door at last and is gone.

'Talk to me!' Sohrab calls.

───

When I wake in the morning, my breakfast is waiting on the tray. I didn't hear them sliding it under the door. I get to my hands and knees, and force myself across the floor, but every movement I make sends pain shooting through me. It amazes me that my body can report pain from so many distinct places. In the night, it was all like one great block of pain, but now each joint in my body sends a different message of pain; my fingers, my knees, my ankles, my hips, my shoulders and neck, my backbone. I have thickened everywhere – thick tongue, thick eyes, thick face, my limbs themselves feel thick and throbbing, and my lips are so thick that I can see them sticking out when I glance downwards.

I swallow the breakfast food without chewing anything, and tilt my head back so that I can pour the water straight down my throat.

'Talk to me!' Sohrab shouts.

'I'm all right!'

'Are you okay?'

'Yes!'

'Talk to me!'

I let him go on calling, but make no more attempts to call back to him. It's almost as if he's trying to add to my misery. He's not, I know that. He's worried, but I'm sick of him.

I lie flat on my back on the stinky blanket and, millimetre by millimetre, make my eyelids close.

I think: *If they really were going to send me home, they'll change their minds now.*

I think: *All those cells!*

The water I have just poured down my neck has gone straight to my bladder. I will have to put the green slip out. My pain and misery make me sob, but there are no tears, just an unbearable stinging in my eyes. Enough! Can't I even swallow water without inviting more pain?

I push the green slip under the door with my foot, and wait for the blindfold. I want to tell them that there's no need for it – I can't see anything.

The blindfold is dropped in through the slot and I struggle to get it over my head and eyes. I have to use the back of my wrists to push it into position because the joints of my fingers won't bend sufficiently.

The door opens, and someone grabs my arm and hauls me upright. It's not the woman. It might be the guard who beat me last night. He supports me down the corridor.

'I don't feel sorry for you,' he says. 'You asked for this.'

Back in my cell after relieving my poor bladder, I lie on my blanket and try to work out ways in which I can kill myself if more punishment comes along. It's an important mental project, working out a means to end it all, but at the same time it's futile. There is no way, unless I can bash my head against the wall hard enough to fracture my skull, but that's very unlikely. There's nothing in here to hang myself from. I can't stab myself to death with a spoon. If I tore a piece of my blanket and jammed it down my throat, would that choke me? But how would I tear the blanket? You need hands and fingers and strength in your muscles to do that.

The only blessing I have is that the pain makes me pass out every so often.

Sohrab, at least, has stopped calling down to me. He's screaming about Leila again – how he intends to strangle her with his bare hands when he gets out.

Night comes. Evening prayers. In the cells all over Evin, people are kneeling in prayer. The guards are kneeling in prayer, too. They are all praying to honour the same God.

I nurse my pain all through the night. I don't faint now. The fainting is gone.

In the morning, after Azan, the cell door opens. It's the female guard with a male guard, not the one who beat me before. The male guard gets down on his knees and starts punching me as hard as he can. He pulls my hands away from my face, and aims punches at my mouth. He uses his elbow to gouge my chest and stomach. I don't scream. I try as best I can to shield my face. I can hear Sohrab shouting at the guards, 'Leave her alone, you arseholes!'

'That's enough,' says the female guard. 'Let's go.'

The guard stops beating me immediately. He's not as motivated as the guard who first beat me.

I am lying so still that I can't be sure whether I am alive or dead. This might be exactly the way that people feel when the life leaves their bodies. Not a single motion. But what about the pain? The dead wouldn't have to endure pain, or what would be the benefit of death?

Sohrab calls down to me, 'How is the little champion?' He's making a pun on my name, 'Ghahramani', which means 'champion'. It's a weird thing, but these latest blows to my face have freed my mouth a little. Maybe it will be worse than ever in a few minutes, but just for now I can open and close my jaw. Is it the adrenalin?

I push myself up to a sitting position with my back against the wall.

'Sohrab?'

'So you're alive?'

'No.'

'Do you mean you're dead?'

'Yes, I'm dead.'

Sohrab laughs in delight. This is the sort of comment that he loves.

'Little champion!' he says.

'Not a champion. This fight isn't fair. I won't win this one.'

He laughs again, even happier with this comment. He has something else to say, something complicated, but my respite from pain is over. It comes into my face and my ribcage with such frightening ferocity that I fear I will split open.

I pass out.

—

The rest of the day passes with me waking, attempting to move, then fainting again. It happens maybe four or five times. No matter how bad I feel, if food is waiting for me on the tray I crawl over and push it into my mouth, and I drink the water. I don't properly understand why I do this, unless it's a type of primitive urge of the body to repair itself, overruling a lack of interest.

I don't have to worry about finding a way to kill myself. If they beat me again, I know I will die. If I could do anything to avoid another beating, I would, without a second's hesitation. The female guard from the south with the burnt-away face: whatever she wants to do, she can.

—

On the third day since my first beating, I find I can sit up against the wall without fainting. I always sit facing the door. If it begins to open, I intend to say a prayer for my mum and my dad and my brothers and sisters, then give in, and it will all be over.

On my last two visits to the toilet, I haven't seen anything of the female guard. I have seen both of the male guards who beat me, though. They don't mention anything about the beatings. It wouldn't surprise me if they have forgotten about them.

My lips are healing and I can see a little better. My tongue stings, but I can move it about in my mouth. My fingers are almost as good as new. I keep touching my teeth with my fingertips, assuring myself that they are there. If it should happen that I get out of here and get better, I want to be able to smile at people and hear them say, 'Well, you still have your lovely smile, I see!'

'When are you going home?' Sohrab asks me.

'I don't know.'

'What will you do if you have to stay here?'

'I'll die.'

'Do you think so?'

'I know.'

'Many people believe that, Zarah. There are people here who wanted to die five years ago.'

'What did you think when you knew you would be here forever?' I ask Sohrab. I don't really care what he thought, but the sound of his voice helps me, for a short time, to let go of the bleakness and despair inside me.

'I wished I had killed a few of them before I ended up here. It would've given me pleasure to think of them dead and to know that it was because of me.'

'Is that all?'

'That's a lot.'

'I would be worried for my family. My mother would die.'

'People forget you after the first sunset.'

'Don't you dare say that!'

'It's true. Alas.'

He has made me angry. If I could get at him, I'd slap his stupid face.

'Maybe people forgot about you because you're mad. My mother and father will never forget about me. Never in a million sunsets. You don't know what it's like to have a child you love. Nobody can forget their daughter or their son.'

'Whatever you say.'

I stay silent for a time. I hate Sohrab for thinking that about my dad and mum. If I couldn't think of them, I would have nothing. Even though they're not here, they are keeping me alive as surely as if they were spoon-feeding me with soup, and bathing me with warm water.

'That's something they haven't taken away from me,' I say to Sohrab when I'm ready. 'I believe in my mum and dad. Forever.'

'Princess,' he says, 'they don't care about your mum and dad.

They don't care about anything. Nothing.'

'They cared about my ideas. That's why I'm here. They care about what I say and what I write.'

'No, Zarah. Your ideas are of no interest to them. They put you in here because you were disobedient. In a week or so, they might change their minds about what people can do and can't do. All that matters is that you do what they say, whatever it is. That's good enough for them.'

'People have been killed in here for their ideas,' I tell Sohrab hotly. 'How dare you say they don't care!'

'Nobody kills anyone because of ideas,' he says. 'You kill people because you realise they don't need to be alive any longer. That's all.'

I refuse to go on with the conversation. Sohrab apologises, but I don't answer him. I have nothing to say that can counter his cynicism, but I know he's wrong. Or, if what he says is true, then okay … but other things are also true. I lie still with my eye on the door, thinking over all the things that have happened in the last two years. The memory I am most content with is that of listening to a famous Iranain film-maker when he came to show one of his movies at uni to students like me who'd been shouting in the street. After the movie – *Deep Breath*, it was called – someone in the audience told the film-maker that nothing would change by making movies about our problems, and that much more was needed.

The film-maker said there was a time when he was studying cinema that it was illegal to have a video player at home, and he had to buy one, in exactly the way that people buy drugs today. He had to be able to see movies from all over the world if he was going to make movies himself. His parents, though, called the Basij to tell them that their son had a video player. At that time, he said (and he was talking about the years just after the Revolution in 1979), people could only think in one way.

So movie-makers like him ended up in jail – and writers, too, and artists, and businessmen, and academics. But when they got out of jail, these people persisted. They made their movies, they wrote their books, they made their speeches, and they opened their businesses that sold such things as video players. So things changed a bit, the film-maker said, and so now there was not just the one way of thinking; there were one-and-a-half ways of thinking, and one day there would be two ways, then two-and-a-half. And the guy in the audience who'd said that trying to change things with movies was a waste of time said, 'Or maybe we'll go from one way of thinking to less than one way.' The film-maker said, 'Maybe. But do it anyway. Make the movies, write the books.'

In the night, I hear Sohrab calling for the guard to take him to the toilet. He doesn't bother with the green slip; he just shouts out. I heard him coming back from the toilet, laughing and swearing at the guard, calling him an arsehole. And I think, *Oh, God, no!* I know they will come and beat him, and they do. There are at least two of them beating him, and he shrieks with laughter while they go about it, and screams abuse. 'Arseholes! Stupid cunts!' I put my hands over my ears and make as loud a sound as I can to block out the beating and swearing; by the time they are done with Sohrab, I am a quivering wreck.

'Not bad,' says Sohrab, still heaving. 'I exhausted them that time. Did you hear?'

'Of course I heard, you imbecile! I hate you! You're sick!'

'You think so?'

'I hope you die one day when they're beating you!'

'Might happen.'

'You should be in a mental hospital!'

'In a mental hospital? I thought I was!'

I can't stand him in this mood. Sometimes I love him and want to take care of him and tell him stories. And sometimes, like now, I want them to take him out and shoot him.

chapter twenty-four

I sleep fitfully, knowing that tomorrow is the day I am supposed to be freed. My ability to keep track of time in here has improved over the weeks. So, tomorrow. But will they keep their word? Will they release me, as they said they would? I mustn't let myself believe that honour has anything to do with their thinking. I must make these past twenty-nine days count for something more than pain and humiliation.

I have seen my enemies up close, and now I know things about them I didn't know before. I must never forget what I know about my enemies. My life is precious to me, but it isn't precious to them. The world itself is precious to me, but the world isn't precious to them. If I awake on a spring day and dress and walk out under the trees and see the patterns of sunlight shifting on the ground, I feel a joy that makes me want to smile at every stranger I see. But they don't see the sunshine, and spring means no more to them than another season of enforcing their will, of rewarding the obedient and punishing the disobedient. And they feel no desire to smile at strangers. A stranger to them is no more than a person whose allegiance has not yet been studied and catalogued. They save their smiles for those who have no questions to ask; for those who pass Evin and think to themselves, *God approves.*

I lie wrapped in my stinky blanket, feeling the bruised and damaged parts of me for small signs of healing. I touch my lips with my fingertips, gently test my eyelids and the swelling below my eyes, move my tongue in my mouth to see if the stinging is less than it was, reach down and pat my ribcage, flex the muscles in my legs, and judge the protests coming from the purple shapes that show the darker impression of the guard's knuckles. Five days after the beatings, I can walk and talk and see, and no bones are broken. 'Could've been worse,' I say, and grin despite myself. I am beginning to sound like my madman, who is such a connoisseur of beatings.

Very early, when morning prayer is barely over, I hear a sound at my door. I flinch and wait. I haven't forgotten my promise to myself – that if they come to beat me again, I will pray quickly, bless my mother and father and brothers and sisters, and die. But the door doesn't open. Instead, a bundle is forced through the slot and falls to the floor. I remain where I am, still expecting something more – something worse – but a count to one hundred passes without the door opening. I go to the bundle and spread it open. They have given me back the dress I was wearing when they brought me here: just a plain, black, cotton dress, almost ankle length.

I kneel with the dress pressed to my face, and my tears begin to flow. I can smell myself on the fabric! I can smell the person I used to be! Oh, it goes to my heart like a blade! It's Zarah, that poor, foolish girl whose life was all laughter and kisses and daydreams and hopeful petitions! Oh, God, just remembering her makes me want to slap her face and tell her to wake up! *Oh, Zarah, you silly thing; you poor, stupid, lovely girl!*

My face soaking wet, I pull on the dress and smooth its wrinkles. Then I stand at the back wall and wait, the blindfold around my forehead ready to pull down over my eyes.

A guard hits the door with his fist – the signal to cover my eyes. He will wait two minutes, then open the door. I call up to Sohrab, 'Are you awake? I'm going home.' He answers straight away; I think he has been waiting.

'Safe journey,' he says.

'I'll put flowers on your mother's grave. Marguerites, like you said.'

'That would be good. Thank you.'

'I'll remember you!'

'Until sunset,' he says, and laughs.

The guard opens the door. He takes hold of my arm and says, 'Let's go.' At the lift, he hands me over to someone else. I don't know who; the voice is not familiar. But he may have seen me before, whoever he is, because he says to the guard, 'Haven't you been feeding her?' and chuckles. He turns me around and quickly binds my wrists behind my back with what feels like a plastic strip.

I am taken down in the lift to a car, just as I was six days ago when I went to court. Once in the car, the man who has been escorting me says, 'Lie down,' and so I do, flat along the back seat with the top of my head jammed up against the door. There's a second man in the car, probably the driver. He greets the man who has charge of me, then I am left on the back seat while the two of them travel in the front.

It soon becomes obvious to me that we are not travelling along the same route we took to court. I can hear more traffic sounds, many more, and I can hear the early-morning shouts of people in the street. The voices are just those of ordinary people.

I hear a man calling out the price of his pretzels, and another man crying out, 'Back it in! Not forward, not forward!' I hear the sound of a mother scolding a child about something or other, and the cursing of drivers, and horns sounding impatiently. It is as if the world is seeping back into me, soaking down into places that have been arid for a month.

The car travels slowly for a long way, lurching in and out of the traffic and stopping and starting again. I get thrown about on the back seat, not having my hands free to steady myself. My nose is pressed into the vinyl of the upholstery.

After what seems an hour or more, the car breaks free of the traffic and accelerates. One of the men in the front seat, the driver, says, 'Thank God for that!' and the other, the man who has charge of me, says, 'It's worse every year. They've gotta do something.' And the driver says, 'Not in our lifetimes, Haji!'

Now the car is speeding along what must be a highway, judging by how smoothly we are travelling. Wherever they are taking me, it is not to my father's house. We could have reached my father's house in twenty minutes from the gates of Evin. Of all the possibilities for our journey's destination, a grave in the wastes outside Tehran seems to me the most likely. Before my prison days, I heard rumours of cars and trucks being seen in the wastes for no reason, and of areas closed off, perhaps because those areas were dumping grounds for dead trouble-makers. I found those rumours hard to believe then, but I don't now. Anyway, if they intend to shoot me, that is the best of the possible outcomes. Transferral to another prison is one of the worst.

If I am put into another prison, I will find a way to kill myself. I won't wait days and days to do it – I'll be as quick as I can. I write a letter in my head to Mum and Dad, in case this should be the end of me. I tell them both how much I've been missing them, and thank them for my life. Because Mum has a strong belief in rebirth and things like that, I tell her that I will be somewhere waiting, but I feel embarrassed to be going on in this way. Still, it is for her, and haven't I always found sweet things to say just because it's what she loves?

After a long period of no traffic noise and no conversation between the driver and the man in charge, the car starts to slow down. The driver says, 'Here?' and the man in charge grunts. The car comes to a halt and both doors open. I can hear a sound I can't work out at first, then realise that one of these two men is urinating on the ground right outside the back door of the car. He must be having bladder problems, because he keeps stopping and starting and grunting.

The door against which my head is jammed opens, and my head is left dangling. The man in charge says, 'Okay, get out.' I struggle upright then feel with my foot for the door opening. Now I'm standing, unsteadily, all of my bruises throbbing from lying awkwardly on the seat. I can feel open air on my face. The plastic strip on my wrists is cut, and my hands fall to my sides. I hear the two car doors thud shut; I hear the engine start. I am baffled – more baffled than fearful. What, in heaven's name, is going on?

The car starts to roll away, crunching what must be the stones on the verge of the road. Then it stops again, and a door opens. Once more, I hear the sound of urine splashing on the ground. Either the one who didn't pee before has decided he must relieve himself, or the one who groans when he pees is finishing off. I hear the groan I heard before. A voice calls, 'You want me to drive, Haji?' There's no answer. The door slams, and the car drives away.

I wait where I am, standing completely still. I wait until I am absolutely certain that the car has gone. I hear no other cars at all. I hear nothing but the rush of the cold wind. I reach up and pull off the blindfold.

The vastness of the empty land around me makes me gasp. I am nowhere. A paved highway stretches a long way ahead. Looking back the other way, I can dimly make out a grey smudge in the distant sky that must be the smog of Tehran. There's not a building to be seen; not even a shack. The pale blue sky is gigantic — it stretches so much further than I recall from the past. Dry hills that are the colour of bone stand away to the west. I shield my eyes and blink up at the sun, then turn slowly in a circle. The land is blank.

I begin to walk back in the direction of Tehran. It will take a long, long time to walk the distance. If I hear a car, I will hide, although where I would hide is difficult to say. Being free again is not what I'd thought it would be. I had imagined that I would leap like a lamb in a paddock, and shout at the top of my voice. But I have no desire at all to leap; no desire to shout. I feel exposed, and wish that the road had trees along the side so that I could duck in and out of cover. I am still carrying my blindfold. Hated though it is, I can't throw it away. I clutch it tight in my fist and march into the wind, holding my headscarf in place with one hand.

When I hear the first car approaching from behind me, my heart stops, and muscles all over my body tense themselves. It speeds past me without the slightest acknowledgement; a bright red car, brand new. I glimpse a woman in the passenger's seat with her hair uncovered; the driver's trophy wife or girlfriend, exercising her freedom where there are no Basij or policemen to make a fuss. Cars come from the other direction, heading away from Tehran, and each time they approach me I tense up. The people in the cars must think me a malnourished peasant girl, probably crawling with lice and with bad teeth behind cracked lips. I have seen girls that look as I do now when I've been driving out into the countryside with Behnam. I always thought, 'Poor thing!' and then chastised myself and said, 'It is only by God's grace that you are not her.'

My long, dogged march brings me to the first buildings I have seen this day. I stop to gaze down at the few ragged shops and shoddy dwellings of concrete brick. I know where this is. This is Ekbatan, the most outlying suburb of Tehran. For the first time in a month, I have my bearings. The map of my life begins to re-emerge from the drabness within me. Colours grow more vivid; blurry lines now stand distinct. I have driven through here with my father, and with Behnam on outings to the countryside. I have looked with pity at the dreariness of this street that seems to me now a grand boulevard, as welcome a destination as the famous boulevards of great cities I have yet to visit.

I walk until I see a phone booth just to the side of the road. I have no coins, and will have to ask passersby for the money to ring my father. I stand on the sidewalk practising smiles so that my hideous appearance will be less of a fright to those who might come along. Down the road, I see an old man approaching slowly with two loaves of bread under his arm and a newspaper in his hand. He glances at me, and I offer him my grotesque smile. He stops and gazes at me with puzzlement in his eyes. I can imagine how shocked he must be at my appearance. My head had rubbed against the inside of the car door when I was being driven here, and scabs were torn away. Trickles of blood have dried on my forehead and cheeks. And the old man must be studying my bruised eyes, my broken lips, my stick-like wrists and dirty hands.

'What is it, miss? What brings you here?'

'Would you have a coin for me? I want to make a phone call.'

'A phone call?'

'Yes. It's important.'

He puts his paper under his arm with the two loaves, and reaches into his pocket. He pulls out a leather pouch, unhurriedly feels inside it, and hands me a coin. I am still smiling in my hideous way.

'Miss, are you unwell?' he asks me.

'No,' I say, but I see the doubt in his eyes and amend my answer. 'I fell over.'

He nods his head, plainly unconvinced.

'You should sit down, miss. Over there in the park.'

I look in the direction of his gaze and see a small, grassed area and a struggling tree on the opposite side of the road between a half-finished building and a yard where concrete pipes are stored on top of each other.

'I will,' I tell him.

'Would you like some bread?' he says.

'You wouldn't mind?'

'Why should I mind?'

He tears one of his loaves and hands a half to me. It is bread of the sort I have always loved, the crust all bubbled and sprinkled with sesame seeds. The aroma of it would be enough by itself to make me drunk.

'Be sure to rest,' the old man says, and nods his head, as if to reinforce the good sense of the advice he is offering me.

'I will rest, certainly,' I say.

As the old man continues on his way, I hurry to the phone

booth, praying that it will be one that works. I put in the coin, and hear a healthy dial tone, to my great relief. I dial my home number. I know by the light in the sky that it is about eight in the morning. My father will not have left for his shop in the bazaar yet.

My father's voice flows into my ears. 'Ghahramani household,' he says.

'Agha Jun?' I say – my way of addressing my father. 'It's me. It's Zarah.'

I hear a cry, almost a shriek of pain. 'My baby, where are you?' He is talking in Kurdish, the most natural tongue for him, and his most intimate. 'I will come. I will come now. Where are you?'

'Ekbatan, block 31. I'm in a phone booth. There's a little park and a pile of pipes, big pipes. I'll wait there.'

My father has to ask me to repeat what I've said. He is crying loudly and seems unable to stop himself. I tell him again, and a third time. In the background I can hear my mother pleading again and again, 'Is it Zarah? Oh, God, is it her?'

'Don't leave where you are,' my father says. 'I am coming now. Baby, you must not leave where you are.'

'I won't, I won't!'

My mother's voice is on the line now, but only for a second before my call expires. All I hear is, 'Precious . . .' in Kurdish.

I replace the receiver and walk across the road to the little park.

The sound of my father's voice, and my mother's for that bare second, has flooded me with joy. I sit on the seat wailing aloud and wiping tears from my cheeks. Then I glimpse the bread in my lap, and I stop crying and feed chunks of it into my mouth. Between mouthfuls, I give myself over to wailing again. If I were

246

in paradise, this is what I would wish it to be: fresh bread, tears of joy, and my mother and father hurrying to me.

I clutch my blindfold tightly in my free hand.

acknowledgements

The authors would like to express their gratitude to Ann Dillon for her help and suggestions during the creation of the manuscript, and for her valuable research.

All the members of Zarah Ghahramani's family are especially acknowledged for their patience and loving support; and her secondary school and university teachers are asked to accept her gratitude, for reasons that will be apparent to any reader of this book.